SUCCESS IS A MOVING TARGET

Other books by Robert A. Raines

To Kiss the Joy
Lord, Could You Make It a Little Better?
New Life in the Church
Reshaping the Christian Life
Creative Brooding
The Secular Congregation
Soundings

SUCCESS IS A MOVING TARGET

ROBERT A. RAINES

WORD BOOKS, PUBLISHER
WACO, TEXAS

Illustrations by
GLORIA EVANS

SUCCESS IS A MOVING TARGET
by Robert A. Raines

Scripture quotations marked RSV are from the Revised Standard Version
of the Bible, copyrighted 1946 (renewed 1973), 1956 and © 1971 by the
Division of Christian Education of the National Council of the Churches
of Christ in the U.S.A. and used by permission.
Scripture quotation marked TEV is from *Good News for Modern Man,*
the Today's English Version of the New Testament, copyright © American
Bible Society 1966, and is used by permission.

Grateful acknowledgment is made for the quotation from THE PEOPLE,
YES by Carl Sandburg, copyright, 1936, by Harcourt Brace Jovanovich,
Inc.; copyright, 1964, by Carl Sandburg. Reprinted by permission of the
publishers.

Grateful acknowledgment is made also for "What Can I Tell My Bones,"
copyright © 1957 by Theodore Roethke, from THE COLLECTED POEMS
OF THEODORE ROETHKE. Used by permission of Doubleday & Company, Inc.

Library of Congress catalog card number: 75–10091
Printed in the United States of America

To my son Bob

Contents

Introduction

One of the dilemmas of my life has been the struggle to be both successful and Christian. I haven't been quite able to settle for either by itself, if either were attainable. If neither self-denial nor do-your-own-thing is an adequate expression of a Christian style of life, how are we to relate our oughts and our wants? It is our burden and our freedom that there is no single articulation or interpretation of

Christian living that fits all of us any of the time or any of us all of the time. Our goals change. Our self-understanding changes. Our understanding of Christianity changes. So each of us must search out his own definition or direction of success in the light of the Biblical perspective as he perceives it, and in the context of his own life's unfolding meanings.

This book is a modest effort to share some of my own learnings in exploring what it means to be a successful person, congregation, nation, and Christian. It is not a "how to" book, but a "how through" book. Success through failure, winning through losing, healing through wounds, life through death, hope through despair, laughter through tears, courage through fear, joy through pain.

The six chapters in the book raise questions about our success targets, and are designed to assist you in getting a bead on where your targets are moving.

Robert A. Raines

SUCCESS IS A MOVING TARGET

Chapter 1

What does it mean to be a

successful person?

BECOMING
A NEW CREATION

In his book *The American Idea of Success,*
Richard Huber wrote:

> In America, success has meant making money
> and translating it into status, or becoming
> famous. . . . It was not the same thing as
> happiness—which is how you feel. It recorded a
> change in rank, the upgrading of a person in

13

relation to others by the unequal distribution
of money and power, prestige and fame. . . .
Success was not simply *being* rich or famous. It
meant *attaining* riches or *achieving* fame. You
had to know where a man began and where
he ended in order to determine how far he
had come.[1]

In America, success means making it in terms of
money, power and fame. And as the Swedish
sociologist Gunnar Myrdal is reported to have said,
"Americans worship success." So the cross of Jesus
may be a less accurate symbol of what we in fact
worship than, say, a solid gold Cadillac—or in
today's energy crisis, a solid gold Volkswagen!

It reminds me of the story of the rich man who
decided that when he died he wanted to be buried
in his gold Cadillac. The word got around and when
the day came, the crowds gathered to watch as the
gold Cadillac was slowly lowered by a crane into
the grave. And sure enough, there he was—the
dead man in the driver's seat, white-gloved hands on
the wheel. As the Cadillac was slowly lowered into
the grave, one bystander was heard to whisper
to another, "Man, that's livin'!"

So what's living and what's dying? What is
success and what is failure? What does it mean to

14

be a successful person, nation, congregation, Christian? I propose in this first chapter to explore what it means to be a successful person from a biblical perspective. As a mode of exploration, I offer a statement, a question, and a possibility.

First, the statement: Success is a moving target. Months ago a friend sent me a book entitled *The Changing Success Ethic,* published by The American Management Association. It is a report of a survey of several thousand businessmen. It indicates that the American idea of success may be moving away from the accumulation of material goods to the realization of less tangible objectives. "One observer believes that the newly emerging success-related values now favor above material well-being 'the richness of human experience and the rewards inherent in a social reality in which genuine opportunities for self-expression are nearly limitless.'" [2] The success target may be moving toward personal fulfillment. Is that true for you?

In a recent workshop on the success question, there was wide agreement that success *is* a moving target and that our goals change by reason of age, circumstance, growth and events. One woman said, "Success means having my teenagers turn out well. I find that I measure my success in terms of my

children." Another woman said, "Success for me
is finding the best direction for my life now that my
role as mother is ending." Yet another woman said,
"Success for me is being totally fulfilled as a person,
not only wife or mother but also artist—a creative,
thinking person who affects events and people, who
has a sense of worth and recognition." Success is
a different target at this time for each of those
women, and moving for all of them whether they
recognize it or not.

Several clergy in the workshop were saying,
"I've had a terrific lay-on of responsibility and
have felt a tremendous sense of obligation all my life;
and so for me, self-fulfillment and meeting my own
needs and wants is where the target is moving.
From vocational goals to personal goals, that's
where success is moving for me."

A young man in the workshop had his own
successful business, and has left it to work now with
Indians at a considerably lower income. He
said, "Success in my life is contingent upon my
enabling others to identify success in their lives. If
those to whom I have committed my energies don't
see themselves as successful, then I cannot feel that
I have succeeded." For this young man, personal
fulfillment in terms of helping other people is the

important thing now rather than making money. Ten years from now, the target may have moved again for that young man.

His present definition of success would make a good success-target for parents, too: to encourage our children to seek what the moving target of success might mean in their lives instead of laying our targets on them.

For many Americans, especially men, success is identified with work. It's ironic that we get a classic statement of the Protestant work ethic from a Jew, Arthur Miller. He said one time, "I'm not happy in the sense that there are no problems but I'm always happy if I'm working. I'm a person who has never known how to take a vacation so all life is either work or a preparation for it. To be fruitful is to be happy. You don't have to feel you've got the tiger by the tail. It's when you can't find the tiger that the agony begins."

I sense a quiet agony among many people who can't find the tiger and who are out looking for the tiger, and who will admit that having "made it," they haven't "got it made." People who are on the make for a little more meaning in their lives.

At lunch recently, a group of men gathered to talk about this matter of success. Suddenly one man

17

looked us in the eye, directly, forcefully, and said,
"Do you feel yourself to be successful?" I sensed a
slight uneasiness in the air for a moment. Perhaps
it was just me, but I don't think so. Too quickly,
too eagerly, one by one, we all said "Yes." While I
was feeling that a more honest response might have
been "Yes, but—" or "Yes, in this respect, but no,
in that respect" or "I'm not sure any longer what
success means for me."

If you have a job, do you feel that you are
successful in it? If your spouse has a job, do you
feel he or she is successful in it? Do you talk about
these things together?

Like most institutions today, the institution of
marriage is suffering severe pressure. The incidence
of divorce is rising, especially at middle age. Courses
and groups for the enrichment of marriage and the
encouragement of divorced persons proliferate.
Attitudes are fluid and mixed. A young pastor told
me that recently a long-time member of his church
said he was leaving the church because "when I
look out over the congregation on Sunday morning,
there are too many divorced people." While such a
pejorative and hardhearted attitude still permeates
much of organized religion, there are signs in
congregations here and there of more humane and

18

compassionate concern for persons in marital trauma
or divorce. People who were broken, hurt, or had
offended society were drawn to Jesus because he
offered them hope and courage to put their lives
together again.

There are no unchanging road maps. Couples are
searching in fear and hope to find their own way to
live their needs, wants, oughts and loves. Henry
Miller comments, "Love in marriage must be a
constant re-creation of that which caused it to
happen in the first place, namely, expanding one's
mind, ungreediness, self-knowledge, a little of the
public be damned, a willingness for tears, a sense
of ending."

If you are married, how successful do you feel
your marriage is? Do you discuss this kind of thing
with your spouse? If you are not married, are you
working with a satisfying success target for yourself
as a single person, or are you beleaguered with the
notion that you can't be successful alone?

What is success for you? Where is the target
moving for you? Do you feel an inner tug, pull,
nudge, ache, yearning, some sense that it's getting
away from you again?

Paul gave a biblical perspective pertinent to our
concern when he wrote about becoming a new

19

creation. He said, "Therefore, if any one is in Christ, he is a new creation; the old has passed away, behold, the new has come." [3] And the good news is that there is resident in each of us the creative energy of rebirth. It is latent, seemingly dead, but the power of renascence is there to be awakened and released by the Spirit. It is not a matter of what becomes of us but who we become. It is a death/resurrection matter. So the question is, "What's dying in us?" The answer will give us the clue as to what is being born in us. And if nothing is dying in us, then nothing is being born, either . . . because death and resurrection go together like Good Friday and Easter. As Nietzsche put it, "Only where there are graves are there resurrections."

What's breaking up in you then? What old patterns are tight and don't fit any more? Becoming a new creation is painful and uncertain. It breaks images . . . it breaks your image of yourself . . . it breaks your image of God. In the last few years, I found that my image of what God's will is and how to find it was inadequate for the kinds of decisions I was having to make in my own life. I had been taught that God's will was something objective, out there, that I could go and find, that would come clear to me. And as I looked for it and looked for

it and looked for it, I began to feel more and more
that it was a needle somewhere in that haystack,
and I didn't have a prayer of finding it. And yet if
I didn't find it, I would make some awful mistake,
and how terrible that would be.

I don't believe that any more. Providence for
me is meaningful in retrospect but not in prospect.
I think now that God has set us free to be responsible
to make our own choices and to pay the costs for
them, with our eyes wide open and our feet on
the ground, and that God goes with us, goes before
us, and meets us at every corner; and that there
isn't one option that he has in mind that we have
to find somehow among all those options. We do
the best we can. We make our decisions and choices.
We make mistakes. At every turning and corner,
God is there with us as the images within us break,
helping us to put back the pieces, but now in a new
shape and a new pattern. And with a new tenderness
and a new humility because only those who are
broken or have been broken or are breaking can
really understand what it is that may be breaking
in other people.

A friend wrote me: "I think the failure of the
successful centers on built-in, long-standing goals
that, once attained, don't really solve as fully as

expected all of life's problems. So probably the hopes
have been unrealistic and at least temporarily you
are left with the 'is this all there is?' feeling."

When we are discontent with ourselves as we are
and sense that the old self within us is breaking up
and a new, strange self is appearing; when we can't
find the tiger and see those old targets that we
knew so well how to hit right in the bull's-eye
moving out of range and the new targets not yet
appearing, then it's just possible that this is a
death/resurrection time and that there is power
alive in us toward becoming a new creation.

There are critical periods in our lives when this
kind of break up and break out becomes possible.
Adolescence is such a time; elderescence is, and so
is middlescence. There is a growing awareness of
the significance of mid-life. Generously
speaking, middlescence is from the mid-thirties to
the mid-fifties. It is a time when in one way or
another your head hits the ceiling; or when those
primal energies begin to flow again with fresh
vitality; or when you look at your child one day—
that little girl who has become a young woman—
and suddenly you know that twenty years are gone
and she's gone and you sense the transience of
things; or when you look at yourself and read

between the lines in your face, see your angel-demon, feel a touch of madness and hear the tears in your throat. Whatever brings it on, you begin to feel the earth shaking under your feet.

Years ago I came across a book called *The Middle Age Crisis* by Barbara Fried. As I read it, I kept thinking, "How does she understand me? How does she know what's going on in me?" The wit and wisdom of the book were a delight and comfort to me. The author quoted one woman as saying to a counselor, "Everything that makes life worth living for me is either turning gray, drying up or leaving home." A man said, "I've got some kind of free-floating itch I can't possibly get my fingers on to scratch." [4]

In one way or another, the prescience of death hits us in middle age. The first time a man experiences impotence is a threat like maybe nothing else to a man ("O Lord, hit me if you must, but not there!"). Whatever it is that gets you, all of a sudden you are shaking and trembling. It's OK to tremble. Trembling is awe of our being in the presence of the holy. It is God who sometimes causes us to tremble, tremble. When we tremble, we are vulnerable, supple, open to the Spirit. Erik Erikson, the psychoanalytic historian, describes

23

this mid-life crisis as the tension between generativity
and stagnation.[5] It is a threatening/promising
time, a time of the breaking of images (which are
usually idolatrous, anyway), and a time when we
are required to reperceive ourselves, a Nicodemus [6]
time when the potential for creativity and destructivity rises like yeast within us; a time of personal,
professional, marital, and faith appraisal.

Where is that success target moving for you now?
How are your values shifting? What's breaking
down in you? What's being born? Who are you
becoming?

First, the statement: Success is a moving target.
And second, a question: Who gives you your grade?
Who tells you whether or when you are successful?
Who is the present or absentee custodian of your
spiritual values? Parents give us our first grades
and indeed, we may feel their grading for decades
in both positive and negative ways.

In my family, there were three boys. My father
is a bishop (which makes me a son of a bishop!).
All three boys went to theological seminary. It
could be that there was a substantial blast from the
Holy Spirit operating in our family in those years!
It also was the fact that there was a very powerful,
if loving, pressure in our family. That is, if you

really wanted to do what was the best thing, you
knew what that was: you'd be a minister. So we
all went to seminary.

My father was a role model for me for many years.
I adopted his value system without question, both
personally and professionally. I honor it to this day.
But as a result of adopting it without reservation,
I never had a decent adolescent rebellion, much
less an indecent one! Only in recent years have I
consciously begun to own myself and choose my
vocation. I'm glad to be a minister. I like what
I'm doing and I'm glad to be me, but I have realized
in recent years how important it was for me for the
first forty years of my life to please my parents.
I can remember when I had some little victory or
something nice happened, I could hardly wait to
write or phone them because it was such fun to
please them. My parents gave me my grades. And I
wanted all A's.

What expectations did your parents lay on you?
And what expectations have you laid (or are you
laying) on your children? How do you feel graded
by your parents? How do you think your kids
feel graded by you?

My brother Dick is two years younger than I. We
were encouraged in our family context to compete,

and, being older, I almost always won. Dick was
wounded in those years. In order to find and
claim his own selfhood and sense of worth, he's
suffered and searched, and for a time had to
leave the Church in order to experience the power
of the Spirit. He has become, in the rich depths
of his pain and the beauty of magnanimity it yields,
one of the most successful human beings I know.

Some time ago Dick wrote our parents, trying to
explain what was happening to him and in him:

> Whenever people suffer, they must die, be
> reborn, be in a community . . . but this happens
> everywhere, maybe in a church, maybe in a
> family, mostly with help from friends, perhaps
> therapy, perhaps some focused experience of
> nature, of death, love, wherever the depths of
> human experience are touched with love . . .
> there healing takes place. So the Church has
> no corner on the Christ, and Christians have no
> corner on the Christ experience. That is one
> vocabulary of rebirth; there are others. What I
> believe is that the experience of rebirth is
> necessary to a truly creative and free human
> existence. . . . The emotional experience of dying
> and rising are universal, and no one I know who
> has made this journey has ever claimed that he
> could have done it alone. In every case, a

mediator, a community of loving persons are
necessary. Such new birth takes place in the
church, surely, but it is for the church to realize
that it takes place also in a school classroom
or in a neighborhood or in an office. The
community of the church has no corner on
healing or on rebirth. . . . The love of God
within this universe is ever near to all his
creation. Grace is never restricted to church
people. Grace is a fact of life. The strangest
people, the strangest situations, can be the
vessels of communion and baptism. Even in the
midst of evil, the new birth can occur.[7]

Parents give us our first grades and society also
grades us. Society gives us cultural molds which
very largely determine what we think is right and
wrong. A recent commentator noted that men in our
society are not allowed to fail in career but are
allowed to fail in personal relationships, while
women are allowed to fail in career but not allowed
to fail personally as mother and wife. Society stereo-
types our roles, then, and grades us accordingly.

"The customer is always right" slogan may sell
a lot of soap, but it suggests that the yardstick of
value is what will please the client. So it may be
possible to sell a world of soap or religion or
whatever else one is selling, and to lose one's soul in

the process. Society pressures us to give high priority
in our lives to pleasing others. What "pleasing
others" means varies according to our communities
of primary allegiance and need.

There's a lot of pressure in society today to be a
warm, intimate, self-revelatory person. It is good, of
course, to be more personally available to each
other, and I am one of those who in recent years
has been grateful to be broken open and made more
human, more vulnerable, more real. At the same
time, the Kingdom of God is not to be identified
with a constant encounter group. There continues to
be value in privacy, in discretion, and in the
appropriateness of the time and place and persons
involved in self-revelation.

My brother John Raines writes in his book
Attack on Privacy:

> Privacy . . . is a quality of our inter-human
> or transactional lives. It is less "being alone"
> than enjoying the right to determine when and
> how much of oneself is to be known by others.
> Intimacy is not the opposite of privacy.
> *Intimacy is the sharing of privacies.* The
> opposite of privacy is emptiness, resentment, or
> trivialization of inner space, making our
> business everybody else's, or having it made

28

> such. . . . Intimacy is cautious, preserving the distance between selves instead of collapsing it, precisely because it has learned the enrichment of *sharing secrets*.[8]

If one extreme is to be cold and up-tight, the other extreme is to be hot and down-loose. And maybe a golden mean is to be warm and flexible.

A friend said to me that he has noticed in himself in recent years "a move from societal grading to personal valuation." I identify with that move, and believe many people do, perhaps including you. *Inevitably, we grade ourselves.* We choose for ourselves the standards by which we will be graded. This is more than a little frightening because we may be our own most severe judges. Psychiatrist Hugh Missildine said one time, "Sometimes you need to put your arm around yourself." [9] We are taught that we need to put our arms around each other, but sometimes we need to put our arms around ourselves.

Someone said to me, "Success is inside us more than what we achieve out there." Success is being freed from the inside by a self-acceptance which releases the energies of rebirth within us. It allows that ache within us, yearning for release, to flower in strength and beauty.

A woman who has lived for many years with a negative self-image recently experienced a relationship of acceptance. What triggered it for her was a simple hug. It had been years since anybody had hugged her. Anyhow, a simple hug seemed to let something break in her, and she writes about that experience in terms of becoming a new creation. She says:

Life is not a movement over terrain at all.
Its center is standing still in the vortex of
God, which instead of whirling inward, whirls
outward. Growth then is an increasing
awareness, an expansion of the self, the
godliness in us growing and expanding, whirling
outward to new understandings. We are all in
this same vortex, part of the same matter and
yet each separate. I am a part of all I meet
and all that I think upon. I am a part of all
great thoughts ever thought, all great music
ever played and all great dances ever danced.

I ache to know those that exist but that I
have not met. The music of the universe
surrounds me and I ache to know it all. I
hunger for the words of wisdom that are written
and for those not yet written. I ache to whirl
through my vortex and expand to complete
understanding of the universe. But at the same
time I am content to know there is a safe place
inside me, that while it goes everywhere, it
goes nowhere. It just steadily exists day after
day, beaming out love and acceptance.[10]

To be freed from the inside is to follow your own
meaning, to trust your own meaning. I think the
word "calling" may be translated today into the
word "meaning." To trust our own meaning, as

31

authentically as we can understand and
experience it, may be the most dependable way of
hearing the inner resonance of God. To trust your
own meaning is to have the courage to risk living
out of your deepest integrity and to pay the terrible
cost that sometimes makes necessary. To be freed
from the inside is to stand in the vortex of God and
to live out that process of individuation in which
imitating Jesus is not to do literally what he did,
but to live as he did for others out of our own
personhood, out of our own deepest being—to be
and do what is real for us. To be freed from the
inside is to be graded by God whose grade is grace—
amazing grace.

A comment of Paul's that comforts me a great
deal is, "If God doesn't condemn us, who are we to
condemn ourselves?" And yet we do. The title of the
book, *I'm OK, You're OK,* doesn't quite do it for
me. There's something in me that wants to write
another book and call it *I'm an S.O.B., You're an
S.O.B., and It's OK.* There are some not OK
aspects of us and sometimes we feel appropriately
that we are not quite OK. Yet, even in those times
and dimensions, God does not turn his love away
from us. God is able to know us through and
through and love us still and all.

32

Luther, whenever he was in a time of uncertainty or danger, when the things he believed in and counted on were threatened, would say to himself, *"Eo baptismo, Eo baptismo* . . . I am baptized, I am baptized." That phrase reminded him God's love had marked him and would never desert him no matter what. I love the verse of the hymn "How Firm a Foundation" which ends: "That soul though all hell should endeavor to shake, I'll never, no, never, no, never, forsake." God's grace is marked irrevocably and indelibly in our souls, and nothing in all creation that happens to us or that we can do can alter that.

A statement: Success is a moving target.

A question: Who gives you your grade?

A possibility: Failure may be the father of the future. On a recent *Today* show, an MIT professor was describing a course that he offered in 1973 on failure. He said, "Everybody's talking about success, but failure is a far more common experience. It's very important to acknowledge failure and to learn how to cope with it." One of the commentators asked him, "Did anybody fail your course?" He reflected on that for a moment and replied, "No, but there were two Incompletes."

God gives us all Pass/Incomplete. Pass—that

unconditional gracious acceptance, together with
Incomplete—not yet whole, not yet fully grown;
not yet a congruence between the inside and the
outside. Not yet—always not yet. Always becoming.
So it's OK to fail. It's inhuman *not* to fail. It's
frightening if we are unaware of our own failures
because we will then be unable to understand
failure in others.

Someone said, "We need a failure clause in the
contract of life." Humanly speaking, nothing
succeeds like failure. We learn far more about
ourselves in our failures than in our successes.
Failure is the greatest teacher of all. Failure
dramatizes where we are yet incomplete, and points
the way to wholeness. So failure may be the future
signaling to us. The sign of God is that we will be led
where we did not plan to go. In our deaths God is at
work bringing forth resurrection. And in our failures
he is at work preparing us for an unprecendented
and unimaginable future.

Like Jesus on the cross, each of us is victim and
victor in his own process of becoming. There is
something that dies but there is something that is
born. There is a sense in which we are "done to" and
there is a sense in which we "do." We are both
victim and victor in our own rebirth as we become
new creations.

34

For me now, success means the integration of myself. What I mean by that is a congruence of my inside and my outside so that my outside relationships and roles fully, clearly, and authentically express what is real and what is really going on in my inside, so that the inner and the outer person are in focus. I want to be a clear man through and through. I want to have nothing to hide, though much to protect or shelter. I want to be real. I pray that all the intensity of the fire that burns inside me may be allowed to burn brightly, warmly, and appropriately outside in the human community.

And yet as soon as we catch sight of that tiger and get him by the tail, domesticate him and make him a rug under our feet, then it's time to go out looking for a new tiger, a new target, always moving just beyond our reach, and alive in our pain.

We are like Sidney in Lorraine Hansberry's play *The Sign in Sidney Brustein's Window.* Sidney is a very disillusioned man. His little newspaper is about to go broke. His ulcer is kicking up. His wife has moved out and his sister has committed suicide. Wally, the councilman Sidney has backed, turns out to be in the hip pocket of the corrupt political machine. Now at the end of the play, Sidney says to Wally, "I'm going to fight you, Wally. . . . Only

this time . . . we shall be more seasoned, tougher,
harder to fool, and therefore, less likely to quit."
After a brief exchange, Wally says to Sidney, "You
really are a fool." And Sidney replies, "Always
have been. A fool that believes that death is waste,
and love is sweet and that the earth turns and men
change every day and that rivers run and that people
wanna be better than they are and that flowers
smell good and that I hurt terribly today, and that
hurt is desperation and desperation is—energy and
energy can *move* things." That aching energy is
trembling in you and me, urgent towards our
becoming a new creation.[12]

Lord, let us not be afraid of the things that are
breaking in us.
Let us trust that we are still in your hands,
let us be able to trust you in the dark.
We want all the protective devices and defenses
to slide away.
We want to see ourselves real.
Thank you for those aches in us that tell us we
are alive, and that where we hurt we may
yet be healed.
Thank you for that strange grace
that when we are broken and forced out of
hiding,

we discover a great freedom,
a wonderful relief.
Thank you for the people who encourage us to
be real.
Thank you for the people who love us in such
a way
that we are enabled to love them wholly and
fully back.
Thank you for those who deal with us gently
but firmly.
Let our bruises shine.
Strike us with the grace that makes all things
possible
and soothe us with the Gilead balm
that makes the wounded whole,
and shake us til we believe in resurrection,
even our own,
even now.
Amen.

Chapter 2

What does it mean to be a

successful congregation?

LIVING
A NEW VISION

Alfred Stieglitz, one of the great photographers of all time, was on an ocean voyage one time in 1907 in first-class accommodations. He went for a walk as far forward on deck as he could to the steerage. The steerage was a kind of open deck on a ship of that kind where the cheapest passage could be obtained. On the steerage there was no privacy,

no comfort, no cover. Stieglitz recalls, "I stood
alone, looking down, spellbound. . . . The whole
scene fascinated me. . . . I saw shapes related to
each other . . . and underlying that, the feeling I had
about life . . . a new vision . . . held me. The
people . . . the feeling of the ship and ocean and
sky." [1]

He took a photograph of the steerage, and it
moves me still today when I look at it. There's a
mother with a baby in her arms, a ragged shawl
covering her head and shoulders, a clothesline with
some clothes hanging on it. Two old women are
seated on a bench, withdrawn and not talking. You
get the feeling that they are in their mute way
resigned to their condition for the days of this
voyage and indeed for the days of their years.
There are children at play oblivious to the steerage,
like children in a floating ghetto. People are looking
down from the first-class section wearing top hats
and beautiful gowns.

As I recall that picture of the steerage, I feel the
sadness of human life. We're all on the same
journey. Our accommodations vary drastically,
but we're on the same Spaceship *Earth*, floating in
the sea of space.

Sometimes on a street corner or on a subway, I

want to reach out and say to someone, "Hello, stranger. Don't be afraid. Don't be afraid of me. I'm afraid, too. We are all in the same boat together." Sometimes I feel a strange tenderness for strangers whose faces reveal in mute repose the hidden ache in my own heart.

An appropriate caption under that picture of the steerage would be the words that Jesus used from Isaiah to identify his mission—the Christian mission in every time and place, in our time and place: "The Spirit of the Lord is upon me, because he has anointed me to preach good news to the poor. He has sent me to proclaim release to the captives and recovering of sight to the blind, to set at liberty those who are oppressed, to proclaim the acceptable year of the Lord." [2]

What does it mean to be a successful congregation?

Biblically speaking, a successful congregation is one which evokes in its people a compassion for suffering humanity and the courage to do something about it. It is a congregation in which the spirit is alive, opening the eyes of the heart, to see and feel the hurt of humanity. It is a congregation that undertakes the same liberating mission that was the core of Jesus' lifework.

41

The mission of human liberation begins again
and again with a new compassionate vision. The
congregation that would successfully carry out
Jesus' mission of human liberation must be helped
to look upon its immediate world through the lens
of these verses in Luke, and to see and to feel the
human need within range and reach of active
compassion.

There are the poor—those without power,
without resources to cope, without tools with
which to live with dignity and hope. It is one thing
to have problems. We all do. But it's another
thing to have the desperation of not having
resources to deal with problems. There are those
who are poor in self-esteem, unable now to reveal
themselves to another person because when they
tried, they made themselves vulnerable and got
terriby hurt. So they closed up.

The old in our society and congregations are
often poor in the dignity accorded to them. Nancy
Heath, Minister to Older Persons at First
Community Church, shared with friends an
experience when she was taking care of her elderly
and sick mother. In a moment of impatience,
Nancy evidently was perfunctory with her. Her
mother looked at her and said quietly, "Nancy,

don't treat me like a child." And in Nancy's
realization comes our realization that sometimes
we treat people in a less than human way. All
Chinese look alike. All little old ladies look alike.
All old people are alike. The person slips away and
we don't see the human being for a moment with his
private terror and his special claim on our respect.

There are the prisoners—those physically behind
bars, those who are spiritually locked up and the
keys thrown away, those in a geographical cage
from which they can't escape.

One day I opened my mail and found a map of
Franklin County (in which Columbus, Ohio, is
located). It was a census tract from 1970 prepared
by Battelle Memorial Institute and published by
the Housing Opportunity Center of Metropolitan
Columbus. It showed the housing patterns of our
county. The visual impact was powerful because
the racial patterns were in color. The green area
reflected from 0 to 1 percent of black population;
the bright red color reflected from 50 to 100 percent
of black residence.

That bright crimson red covered the central
city, and then all around the city was a golf course
green—the suburbs. It reminded me as I looked at
it that while we've made some progress in the

struggle for racial justice, we have a long way to
go. That's a still photograph of where we are in
Franklin County today. There is a white noose
around that black neck—not unlike the city where
you live, perhaps. The 1974 decision of the Supreme
Court regarding the integration of the Detroit
metropolitan area schools, whatever its intentions,
would seem to guarantee that the black neck of our
inner cities will get blacker, and the white noose
around that black neck whiter and tighter.

There are the oppressed—those physically or
emotionally under someone else's heel of personal
or corporate tyranny; those who are used and used
up in the fierce, competitive struggle to reach
somebody's quota, to fulfill somebody else's
purpose.

In the questionnaire used as the basis for *The
Changing Success Ethic,* more than half of the men
who responded said that they thought it was more
important in terms of their advancement and
promotion to please the boss than to do an excellent
job. Personality was more important than character.
To be able to sell yourself was more important
than honesty. Many people work in a climate in
which they are evaluated and sometimes evaluate
themselves in terms of what they *sell* rather than
how much they're *worth* as human beings.

In these days of rightful and necessary focus on women's liberation, black liberation, youth liberation, and the liberation of the aged, there is a poignant need also for the liberation of white, middle-class, "male chauvinist pig" men. Part of the resentment of the middle class today (and especially white males) lies in their feeling that nobody has adequately recognized *their* particular bondage. To be both a WASP and a male chauvinist pig at the same time is a heavy load. You are a bad guy in spades. You have the feeling that society is on your shoulders, that you have to produce and perform and take care of everybody and make it happen. And yet you feel guilty for having the power or confidence to do those very things, and if somehow you fail, you feel even worse. You are so programmed to produce that you have great difficulty just enjoying life and acknowledging your own needs and being able to cry once in a while as well as keep your square jaw jutted out there day after day. (It may be evident that I have a small vested interest in this particular bondage I have been describing!) Every human being needs some kind of liberation, and we will finally only be liberated together in the cause of human liberation.

The mission of human liberation begins with the conversion of the eyes of the heart, the birth of

a compassionate vision, and vulnerability to the
human landscape of pain and need in which one
lives and moves and has his being. But the
compassionate vision by itself will be dulled and
eventually die if it is not expressed in action.
Biblically speaking, a successful congregation is one
that evokes among its people the courage of their
compassion, the courage to invest themselves
personally and corporately in the mission of human
liberation.

Courage is the will to do what we see needs to
be done. Courage is the will to invest our lives in
others without requiring a guaranteed return.
Courage is the will to pay the cost of compassion.
Courage is the discipline that makes dreams come
true. Courage takes us beyond the conventional,
across borders to uncharted territory where
nobody has a map for us, where there are risks,
where the future is unknown, where we are willing
to make ourselves vulnerable as persons and as an
institution in the mission of human liberation.
Courage is hanging in there when it is much easier
to hang back and be cynical. Courage gives us the
hope of transforming our own lives, of restoring
the soul of America, of healing the wounds of the
world, of humanizing the cities in which we live.

Courage is doing what we can today, trusting in the God of tomorrow—for tomorrow.

How do people in a congregation experience the birth of compassionate vision? How do windows open into the varieties of human need crying to be seen? It happens when one person has the eyes of his heart converted, begins to feel compassion for a few specific human beings, and has the courage to do something about it.

One example of this courage of compassion in the congregation I know best is the prison ministry of First Community Church in recent years. The Ohio Penitentiary is a few miles from the church. One of its prison chaplains brought his dog to a veterinarian, George Norris, who happens to be a member of First Community. George asked questions about the prison and the prisoners; there had been severe riots in the Ohio Penitentiary three years before in which several people were killed. At that time George felt that the prisoners who rioted should be shot, thus reducing the cost of maintaining troublemakers to absolute zero! However, George found himself intrigued by what the chaplain told him. He discovered that there were virtually no entertainment or educational opportunities for men behind the walls in this

maximum security prison. In the weeks that
followed, George arranged for a guitar and singing
group from the church to go behind the walls and
put on a concert. Then he himself led an encounter
group for nine men behind the walls, five of whom
had committed murder. He came to care about Bob
Schatzman and Glenn Mann and other prisoners
he was getting to know. Prisoners became persons
for George.

He began to share his concern with other people
in the church. In the next few months dozens of
persons and families began to participate in the growing prison ministry. Men in the honor dorm who were
allowed outside the prison began to worship at the
church occasionally on Sunday. It was something to
arrive at church on Sunday morning and see that
huge orange bus plunked down in the middle of our
affluent suburban church parking area with the
bald lettering "Ohio Penitentiary." Men and women
began to visit prisoners in the honor dorm two
nights a week. Occasionally on Saturday these
persons brought their children to watch softball
games being played by men from the honor dorm.
Relationships deepened and broadened, and scores
more people became involved.

Then Attica happened in September 1971. Ten

days later we had a service of worship in our
sanctuary on the theme "I was in prison, and you
visited me." A wooden, slatted cell was constructed
and placed on a platform in the center of the worship
area in front of the altar. I preached from within
that cell that day, and the sermon was about Attica
and the Ohio Penitentiary and the prison system
in our nation and state, and prisoners, and the
imperative call of Jesus to minister to them.
Perhaps forty convicts were in the congregation
that morning. Because of the high consciousness
of the Attica event in the nation and in the people
of our congregation, and because the service of
worship was directly geared into that consciousness,
the biblical word had electric connection and
significance, and the sense of the Spirit's powerful
presence was widespread. Some of our people were
offended at this demonstration or proclamation of
the gospel; others were turned on. The prison
ministry grew.

Visits back and forth between men in the honor
dorm and people in our church continued. The
prison band performed twice in our church to
raise money for Christmas telephone calls to their
families—a project called "Holiday Hello." Craft
work done by prisoners was displayed and sold

at the church. An organization began to develop.
So many people were seeking to join the prison
concern group that careful orientation was necessary
for an effective ministry. A special group
concerned itself with and for guards, typically
brutalized and brutalizing people in the prison
system. Careful relationships were developed and
maintained with the warden, the governor of the
state, and the commissioner of corrections. All three
of these people spoke at our church. Because their
perspective was generally for reform and ahead of
the attitudes of the legislature and general
population, we found ourselves in the happy position
of being able to affirm and confirm most actions
taken by these administrators. A legislative reform
group developed in the prison ministry.
Eventually one of those persons was appointed
by the governor to the state task force on prison
reform.

The continuing depth of the ministry was and is
person-to-person relationships. One prisoner was in
a growth group for a period of twelve weeks, a
group that met weekly during that time. At the
end of the final meeting, each person in the group
expressed what the group had meant to him. This
prisoner held up a poster on which he had written
these words: "Twelve weeks ago I thought of myself

as a prisoner. Tonight I think of myself as a human being. Thank you all." Prisoners who typically work for five or ten cents an hour are obviously able to earn very little. One prisoner, a leather worker, presented the congregation on Maundy Thursday in 1972 with a framed leather representation of da Vinci's *The Last Supper.* It cost him in labor and materials over four hundred dollars. What a gift of love to us! A few prisoners eventually joined the church and are living examples in our midst of human beings whose humanity has been recovered and who are making great contributions to those whose lives are touched by them.

The frustrations and disappointments of the prison ministry have been many. On Thanksgiving Day 1972 the prison concern group and men from the honor dorm celebrated a Thanksgiving dinner and worship with their families at the church. One young black prisoner skipped for a couple of hours to visit his family, an action which was prohibited by the prison officials and therefore wrong for him to do. He got back after the bus had left for the prison. He was walking along the street in back of the church; a police cruiser apprehended him; there was a scuffle and the prisoner was shot and killed. Personal inquiries were made about

51

the circumstances of the scuffle and the shooting,
but there was no way to get the prisoner's
perspective on the incident, and no way of
answering the question, "If the prisoner had been
white, would he have been shot?"

In time the warden moved, political backlash
developed in the legislature, and a promising reform
movement got stalled. Many people in the group
lost interest. The obstacles to effective prison
reform seemed great, and sometimes overwhelming.
The prisoner who wrote on the poster, "Tonight I
regard myself as a human being," after exemplary
time, applied for a parole and was turned down
by the parole board four to three. Appeals have
been made to those in authority, but the outcome
uncertain at this writing.

Perhaps the most enduring value of the prison
concern group is that it opened a window for our
congregation to see and begin to care about
prisoners in our city and state. It raised our
consciousness as a congregation; it mobilized our
compassion and gave it handles for effective action.
And it happened because one man had the eyes of
his heart opened to see prisoners as persons, and
hundreds came to share his compassionate vision
and had the courage of their compassion.

52

For every even partially successful story such as
the prison ministry, I could tell a dozen stories of
seedling ministries of compassion which never bore
fruit. The disappointments and failures abound, and
this is to be expected. Task forces or mission groups
are born out of response to a crying human need in
the community. Such needs change, and such forces
and groups flourish and wane, and sometimes the
task for which they came into being is achieved
or appears impossible to pursue. A peace task force,
for example, in First Community Church emerged
during the years of the Vietnam war and served a
very useful service of consciousness-raising in
the congregation during those years. When the
Vietnam war was ended for Americans, that task
force had a less visibly imperative mission to
perform. The targets of human liberation move,
and the structure, effectiveness, and tenure of groups
formed to hit those targets will likewise fluctuate.

With all the sophisticated action training we can
muster, still there is no substitute for one person,
or two or three, who get turned on to a specific
human need and commit themselves to it. Maybe
you are ready to be such a person. Maybe your
congregation is ready again for a fresh mission of
human liberation.

GROWING
A NEW MATURITY

If, biblically speaking, a successful congregation is one which evokes in its people a compassion for suffering humanity and the courage to do something about it, in addition, that congregation must also be a headquarters for the growth and training of people to be enabled for the mission of human liberation. Biblically speaking, a successful congregation is engaged in growing a new maturity.

In William Saroyan's *The Human Comedy*, a fourteen-year-old boy named Homer has a job as a delivery boy in the telegraph office of Western Union in his hometown. The time is the Second World War, and Homer finds himself delivering telegrams to families whose sons have been killed in the war. One day a telegram arrives addressed to his mother informing her that her son, Homer's brother Marcus, is dead.

Mr. Spangler, the head of the Western Union office and a friend to Homer, talks with

him as he prepares to go home with his terrible
news. They take a walk together and pitch a few
horseshoes. And then Homer says, "They're waiting
for me at home now. I know they are. I told
them I'd be home for supper. How am I going to
go into the house and look at them? They'll know
everything the minute they see me."

"Wait," Spangler says. "Don't go home just yet.
Sit down here. Wait awhile." They sit quietly on a
park bench, not talking. And after a while, Homer
says, "What am I waiting for?" "Well," says
Spangler, not knowing for sure whether he is lying
or telling the truth, "you're waiting for the part of
him that died to die in you, too—the part that's only
flesh—the part that comes and goes. That dying
is hurting you now, but wait awhile. When the pain
becomes death and leaves you, the rest will be
lighter and better than ever. It takes a little time.
Be patient with it. You will go home at last with no
death in you. Give it time to go. I'll sit with you here
until it's gone." [3]

Mr. Spangler sitting with Homer is a parable of
the new maturity we seek. The new maturity is
corporate. It is a maturity that we can only find
and create together. It isn't individual fulfillment
for one's self, by one's self. It's a communion that

56

is given and received together "until we all attain
to the unity of the faith and . . . to mature manhood,
to the measure of the stature of the fulness of
Christ." [4]

In our congregations on Sunday morning and
through the week, on a one-to-one basis, in groups,
in all that we do and are together, we sit with each
other until the death in us is gone. There is
something dying in each of us. Each of us hurts
in a particular way and sometimes we can put our
finger on the place where it's sore and sometimes we
can't. But we wait here together for the death to
leave us and we try to be patient with the pain and
stay together until that empty space preoccupied
by death begins to fill up with new life, and we
can go home again. Can you put your finger on
what's hurting you at this time? Can you feel where
you are dying inside? Is there someone to sit with
you until the pain becomes total and death
disappears? Or is there someone who needs you to
sit with him or her until the new life fills up the
empty place?

In our life together we keep a vigil of death and
resurrection day by day, week by week. Elie
Wiesel said that what matters "is the
combination of presence and transformation. . . .

Everything becomes possible by the mere presence
of someone who knows how to listen, to love and
give of himself." [5]

Are there even a few people in your church who
know how to listen, how to love, and how to give
of themselves and to receive the self of another?

Just before Christmas one year our choir caroled
for some of our older members at their homes.
One of these persons wrote, "I just want to thank
you for bringing the choir over to sing Christmas
carols. How I enjoyed it! It was just like bringing
the church to me. It made me feel uplifted. Those
happy faces of the choir! I shall always remember
that day. Will you please give the choir a great
big thank you?"

The routine groups in our church life can be
vehicles of transforming presence. We need many
places of primary belonging in the congregation.
As I was having lunch with a guild group at First
Community Church not long ago, I heard the
women pray for a member of their group who was
in the hospital, and realized that such a guild
group can be and often is for many women a place
where people sit together until the death goes away.
The oldest group in First Community Church is
a men's Wednesday morning breakfast group,
which provides a warm and caring context for

men every week. My experience indicates that
many men need and do not have a primary context
of belonging in their congregation. Periodic
luncheon groups in the context of work do provide
such a place, and are valuable for those who
participate in them.

Sometimes it is useful for the whole congregation
to be invited to experience the transforming
presence in a common group life. Lent provides
such an opportunity. During the period of Lent
in 1972, we decided at First Community Church to
study the Letter to the Ephesians together in
five weekly meetings. People were deliberately
put into groups with others they did not know; there
was a mix of ages and sexes. There was a combination
of Bible study, human potential process, and
personal sharing. At each meeting all the people
who came gathered together for instruction or a
presentation, and then divided into small groups
where they spent most of their time. Each group
was called a Power and Light Company, using
two of the major terms in the Ephesians Letter.
The people in the small groups came to feel a close
sense of belonging and understanding in the course
of these meetings. At the final session, each group
drew a banner poster to express its own unique
character, and what group members had discovered

together. These banner posters were presented and
interpreted at a concluding worship service of all
the groups which was a beautiful and moving
experience. The Power and Light Companies were
a vehicle of transforming presence for our
congregation, and the yeast of that Lenten
experience permeated our congregation for months
to come.[6]

Transformation also occurs through the presence
of persons living or dead, near or distant. We used
to speak of this kind of presence in terms of "the
communion of the saints" or "a cloud of witnesses."
As a child I was encouraged to learn some of the
psalms. One that I learned was Psalm 103.
Recently I have been on a personal journey of
some considerable pain. I have found myself
remembering and repeating the opening verses
of that psalm again and again in this time, to my
deep comfort and encouragement. Do you
remember those verses?

> Bless the Lord, O my soul: and all that
> is within me, bless his holy name.
> Bless the Lord, O my soul, and forget not
> all his benefits:
>
> [none of them fringe]

[and here is a list of the benefits]

Who forgiveth all thine iniquities;
                    [not some, but *all*]
Who healeth all thy diseases;
Who redeemeth thy life from destruction;
Who crowneth thee with lovingkindness
and tender mercies;
Who satisfieth thy mouth with good things;
so that thy youth is renewed like the eagle's.[7]
                    [some benefits!]

I experience the presence of that psalmist today,
I share in the communion of the saints of the ages,
and my spirit is transformed.

In the Jerusalem Bible, the word "tender"
appears three times in Psalm 103, always referring
to the love of God for us:

Bless Yahweh, my soul,

. . . .

and remember all his kindnesses

. . . .

in crowning you with love and tenderness.

Yahweh is tender and compassionate.

As tenderly as a father treats his children,
so Yahweh treats those who fear him.[8]

We are touched with the tenderness of God's
love when we are able to be tender with each other.
So we are the capillaries of God's grace to each
other. There is a difference between gentleness and
tenderness. Gentleness is a kindly action with
respect for the dignity of another, and the restraint
of one's own strength. But gentleness does not
require self-revelation or a broken heart. Tenderness
is born of intimacy and integrity in which one's
self is enabled to reveal himself to another with
all warmth and enabled to receive the other in all
truth. Tenderness occurs in the context of
vulnerability and always triggers a transformation
of some kind. In our fellowship together at its
deepest, everything becomes possible by the
mere presence of someone who knows how to
listen, to love, to give of himself, and to receive
the self of another.

First, the new maturity is corporate. Second, the
measure of the new maturity is Christ. Christ is
the depth and the warmth of our maturity. Christ
is the climate of our community no matter how
clouded we may make it from time to time. Christ
is for us as Christians, not exclusively but
preeminently, the measure of our manhood—the
harbinger of our humanity. He is the clue as to

what it means for us in our time and place
to become fully human in ourselves, for each
other, and to the world.

A friend wrote one time of the man Forbes
Robinson: "A man could not know Forbes for long
and not be quickly conscious of the new sense of
the value of himself. . . . 'He is interested in me'
is what almost every man felt from the start of his
acquaintance with Forbes. . . . 'Pray for him,
believe in him, believe in him, pray for him,' he was
never tired of saying to those who spoke to him
of some disappointing friend. . . . This was the
secret of his extraordinary interest and amazing
belief in nearly every one of us. He saw in all of us,
however ordinary, however commonplace—yes,
however unlovely were our lives—something
somewhere of Jesus Christ." [9]

There is in you and in me something, somewhere,
of Jesus Christ. A gracious part of our new maturity
together is the capacity to see something, somewhere,
of Jesus Christ in another person. And the
capacity to accept and to acknowledge that there
is something, somewhere, of Jesus Christ in one's
own self, too. A way of talking about the deepest
essential focus of one's own being is to say that
Christ is that center and focus. He is in the heart

of our yearning, seeking and struggling to be
fully born and to grow to fulfillment and humanity
as fruit out of its proper vine.

There is also a unique presence of Jesus Christ
in any Christian congregation or institution or
place. Rene Dubos in his book *A God Within* reminds us that *"entheos"* translates into our word
"enthusiasm" and that enthusiasm is the source
of creativity. Dubos notes that "the widespread
acceptance of the words *genius* and *spirit* to denote
the distinctive characteristics of a given region or
city implies the tacit acknowledgment that each
place possesses a set of attributes that determines
the uniqueness of its landscape and its people." He
continues: "Viable human institutions also develop
an inner life, which makes each acquire an identity
and retain it in the midst of change." [10]
I have served three congregations, and each has
its own unique genius and spirit which endure over
a long period of time. The task of congregational
leadership is to facilitate the full expression of the
indigenous genius and spirit in each congregation,
not imposing an external design but rather evoking
the spiritual gifts of that particular people. Dubos
reminds us that Michelangelo in one of his best-
known sonnets expressed a similar feeling about his
task as a sculptor:

The best of artists has that thought alone
Which is contained within the marble shell;
The sculptor's hand can only break the spell
To free the figures slumbering in the stone.

[It is the task of church leadership to free
those parishioners who may yet be slumbering
in the pews, so that the congregation may
truly wake up!]

Dubos gives a beautiful image of the task of
facilitative leadership when he describes the
imaginative care of Eskimo sculptors: "As the carver
held the raw fragment of ivory in his hand, he
turned it gently this way and that way, whispering
to it, 'Who are you? Who hides in you?' The carver
rarely set out consciously to shape a particular
form. Instead of compelling the fragment of ivory
to become a man, a child, a wolf, a seal, a baby
walrus, or some other preconceived object, he tried
subconsciously to discover the structural characteristics and patterns inherent in the material itself.
He continuously let his hand be guided by the inner
structure of the ivory as it revealed itself to the
knife. The form of the human being or of the animal
did not have to be created; it was there from the
beginning and only had to be released." [11]
We are to be sculptors and shapers of our

65

congregations, always asking, "Who are you? Who
hides in you?"—respecting the indigenous genius
and spirit of our given people/place, and, like artists,
rather than manipulating our people for our own
ends, seeking to liberate them to fulfill the purpose
indigenous in their very being. It is for each
congregation to be enabled to discover its own
unique experience of Jesus Christ in its midst. It is
for us as clergy and laity to be sculptors in the
Spirit.

First: The New Maturity is corporate. Second:
The measure of the New Maturity is Christ. And
third: We grow into the New Maturity by growing
into Christ. We talk today about "getting into"
tennis or prayer or music or something else.
"Getting into" something means getting involved in
it, investing ourselves, going deeply into it. So
getting into Christ means growing and going into
the *zone of transformation*. The congregation is the
zone of transformation—the people/place called
First Community Church or St. John's by the Gas
Station, or the name of your church. We are to
expect in the congregation nothing less than
transformation. And at the heart of the zone of
transformation is where the primal energies surge
and where the marvelous becomes contagious. This

is where we sit with each other until the nothing-
ness of death fills up with colors, tastes, sounds
and textures of something new.

A major part of the function of congregational
worship is to provide spokes for all of its people into
the hub of transformation. That is, Sunday worship
must try to be an experience in which any and every
church member can find his place, his room in the
inn. In the early months of 1972 at First Community
Church, we felt in that very diverse congregation
a need for worship and study experiences which
would draw people together and emphasize the
commonality we shared. As we began to think about
the worship theme for the fall, John Carr, at that
time our teaching minister, hit upon the idea of
"homecoming" as a theme. Homecoming rings many
bells: It is the time of coming home to school and
the regular yearly round of activities after the
summer surcease. It is the homecoming of innumer-
able football teams, and there is the resumption of
the regular worship and activity schedule of the
congregation following Labor Day. We gave five
Sundays to an exploration of the parable of the
prodigal son, focusing the first Sunday on the
prodigal, the second Sunday on the elder brother,
the third Sunday on the father, the fourth Sunday

67

on the father's house, and the fifth Sunday (World-wide Communion Sunday) on the homecoming banquet. It proved to be a transforming experience of coming home for many people in our congregation.

Each of us may come into the zone of transformation alone. Albert Einstein speaks of the zone of transformation in these words: "The most beautiful and most profound emotion we can experience is the sensation of the mystical. It is the source of all true science. He to whom this emotion is a stranger, who can no longer wonder and stand rapt in awe, is as good as dead. To know that what is impenetrable to us really exists, manifesting itself in the highest wisdom and the most radiant beauty which our dull faculties can comprehend only in their most primitive forms, this feeling is the center of true religiousness."

You and I are all mystics—though we perhaps wouldn't use that term for ourselves. The most ordinary of us, in terms of sensitivity, has the capacity of a mystic. And sometimes, we become aware of this center of true religiousness, this zone of transformation, this feeling—as in the wonder of a word or a phrase breaking open with fresh meaning and insight to us, or in a moment when we are stunned by an apprehension of truth or beauty or goodness. There is a growing recovery of the practice of meditation in congregations today. Many people are finding various handles and resources for their own meditative processes.[12]

At the heart of that zone of transformation is Christ, God, the Spirit—however you prefer to name that power which energizes each of us to grow into his or her own full humanity.

Dubos writes, quoting Montaigne: " 'There is no one who, if he listens to himself, does not discover in himself a pattern all his own, a ruling pattern which struggles against education.' To live according to this pattern gives us the opportunity to create 'our great and glorious masterpiece.' Indeed, 'to compose our character is our duty.' " [13]

Are you in touch with your ruling pattern—that deepest authentic direction and process of your own selfhood, your inner child of the future struggling to be born out of whatever is your chaos and death? Do you know your own uniqueness? Are you claiming your own existence? It is threatening as well as promising.

Robert Lifton writes: "The Protean experimenter must call forth dark areas of the psyche, demonic imagery of destruction and suffering. . . . These 'death sources' both reflect his dislocation and energize his renewal. While the ordinary person erects protective devices to avoid confronting them, the innovator moves toward them, sensing that his innovation depends upon them." [14]

In the strange alchemy of God's grace, our creativity and our destructivity grow out of the same primal source, energizing our renewal and enabling us in the Spirit to grow and be grown, to know and be known.

The story is told of the dour old Scotsman who was not in church for many Sundays. The pastor of the church went out to see him in his small cottage along a country road. The pastor knocked; the old Scotsman came to the door, opened it, saw the pastor, and without a word motioned him inside. He indicated a rocking chair in front of the coal fire and drew up another for himself. The two men sat in quiet and watched the coals burning brightly.

After a time the pastor stood up, took a pair of tongs, lifted one of the burning coals out of the fire, put it off to the side of the hearth, sat down in his chair and began to rock. Both men watched the lone coal as it grew ashen and cold.

After a time the pastor took the tongs, picked up the now dead coal, put it back in the fire, sat down, and both men watched as once again it burned brightly with all the rest. Without a word the pastor left.

The next Sunday the old Scotsman was in church and never missed from that time forward.

Every coal needs the fire and builds the fire that warms a church that warms a world.

Chapter 3

What does it mean to be a

**DEVELOPING
A NEW HUMANITY**

successful nation?

A recent book by Peter Schrag, *The End of the American Future*, notes that we Americans no longer believe that we have a right to expect better opportunities, progressively higher earnings, and happier, richer lives just because we are Americans. He points out that already in the 1960s many groups were becoming disenchanted with the American dream—blacks, young people, the poor, women, and blue-collar workers. [1]

The new and striking news is that the middle class is becoming significantly disenchanted with the American dream. John Raines has explored middle-class disenchantment in an article in *The Christian Century* entitled "Middle America: Up Against the Wall and Going Nowhere." He writes: "In America today there is not so much a middle class as a class at the top and a class made up of the rest of us who pay the bills . . . less middle-class affluence than middle-class moonlighting, worry and exhaustion." He notes that in 1949, 1 percent of our population owned 21 percent of the total personal wealth of the nation. In 1959, 1 percent of our people owned 30 percent of the total national wealth, and in 1969, ten years later, an astonishing 40 percent of the total personal wealth of this country was still owned by 1 percent.[2] He notes that it is the tax and estate laws which enable the accumulation of this kind of wealth.

He suggests that the takeoff point for "making it" today in America comes at about $25,000 a year, a line which is beyond 95 percent of our people. He says there is a top and that's where the mobility is. And then there are all the rest of us pounding along on

the endless stampede, wondering why we're always
so tired. We're up against the wall and going
nowhere.

This article has now become part of a new book,
Illusions of Success (Judson Press, 1975).

Confirmation and documentation of this analysis
appeared in a new study by Joseph A. Pechman
and Benjamin A. Okner of the Brookings Institution.
Their study concludes that "the overall tax system
does little to alter the distribution of income in the
United States." [3] The study, therefore, rejects the
popularly held idea that the nation's overall tax
burden falls more heavily on upper income groups
and is a generally progressive tax system. Rising
inflation has of course added to the frustration and
anger of the middle class. More Americans than
ever before are asking: Whatever happened to the
American Dream? What's gone wrong? Who is the
villain? What does it mean today for America to be
a successful nation?

A biblical perspective on that question appears in
the second chapter of Ephesians where the author
features the alienation of the Jews and Greeks, who
were separated from one another by walls of
religion, race and nation. It is a classic parable of
alienation. The author says, "God has broken down

those walls of hostility in Christ. He has made us
both one. He is our peace. He is developing between
the two a single new humanity." [4]

While the author of Ephesians is articulating the
purpose of the Church, we can borrow that purpose
as a means of defining from a Christian perspective
what is the measure of a nation's success. We can
say that in the biblical perspective, the purpose of
any nation is to develop among its people through
all their conflicts and diversities a single new
humanity, enriched, chastened, strengthened and
tendered through all that they suffer together in
being made one people. The classic Jew versus Greek
alienation noted in Ephesians 2 is a parable of such
alienated groups in our cultural setting as white
and black, man and woman, young and old, right
and left, etc. Reconciliation means that the survival
needs of each group are honored in a peace without
victory, without the elimination or humiliation
of any.

A successful nation then is developing such a new
humanity in its own life and fostering such a new
humanity in the world. How are we doing in
America? What's happening? What is God doing
with us and in our midst? Let me suggest three
developments.

First, I believe that God is developing a new
humanity in America by enabling us to recover
confidence in ourselves, our institutions, and our
system of government. I find it a strange grace that
two recent events which have greatly disturbed us—
the energy crisis and Watergate—may turn out to
be agents of our recovery of self-confidence. A
theological way to put that is to say that judgment
is the hard form of grace.

Alistair Cooke has written about the energy crisis
in the perspective of American history. "What is
comparatively new in the American experience is
the steady devotion to comfort. We were once the
great, thrifty, tough pioneer country, and now we've
become the most petted nation on earth. Six percent
of the world's population is using up one third of
the world's energy." [5] Suddenly the day of cheap
energy is over for us.

But the response of the American people to the
energy crisis in terms of voluntary thrift has been
encouraging. Such simple expedients as turning
thermostats to 68° or below and accommodating to
a national speed limit of fifty-five miles an hour
have been readily and generally accepted. I sense
not only a ready willingness to cooperate, but even
a tiny little hunger to get committed to something

77

of value for the sake of our country. Even an
eagerness to make small sacrifices together for
America, if it matters, if it's sensible. Many who
were turned off to traditional expressions of
patriotism in the '60s want to find their way back
from cynicism and apathy. While there is then a
dearth of material energy, there may be at the same
time a resurgence of spiritual energy—a fresh
realization that we can and we will cope with our
situation. That maybe we can even *be* more with
less. There may be coming a quiet return to the
pioneer virtues of thrift and self reliance, of the
simple life lived more readily and gladly in the
context of nature.

I make three qualifiers to that hopeful expression.
One is that the poor, the weak, the sick, the old,
and the handicapped, who always suffer most when
there's less of anything around, will continue to need
—even more than before—appropriate assistance
from the rest of us who are healthy and
have resources. A second is that the oil industry
should have its tax depletion allowance depleted!
And a third is an acknowledgment that we may, in
the legitimate need for privacy, be inadequately
sensitive to the danger of privatism. Yet it remains
possible that the movement to natural foods, the
growing rejection of big cars (except Cadillacs

and Continentals!), communal living experiments, the questioning of constant economic growth—while small and inconclusive signs—may signal a healthy mid-life crisis in America.

Watergate, in addition to the energy crisis, may also be an agent of the recovery of confidence in ourselves and in our system of government. We realize in reflection that what has happened represents a failure of particular men, but also celebrates the success of the system. Henry Steele Commager, the distinguished historian, writes:

> The long-drawn-out process of inquiry by committee, by the courts, by the Congress is a stunning vindication of our constitutional system, a vindication of the principle of separation of powers, of the independence of the courts and the foresight of the framers.
>
> The men who made our Constitution were familiar with the history of executive tyranny. . . . They took over the English practice of impeachment, applied it to their highest office, providing a legal and peaceful method of removing the President himself from office.
>
> Thus, in the words of Alexander Hamilton, they "substituted the mild magistracy of the law for the terrible weapon of the sword."
>
> Confronted, for the first time in our long

history, with a chief magistrate who betrayed
his oath of office, we have resorted to that
"magistracy of the law" and vindicated once
again the wisdom of the Founding Fathers.
Thus, we have demonstrated to the world and,
let us hope, to future generations that the
Constitution is alive and well, that it can be
adapted to the exigencies of governance, and
that in an emergency an enlightened and
determined democracy can protect and defend
its principles, its honor, and its heritage.

When, on Sept. 17, 1787, members of the
Federal Convention came forward to sign the
Constitution that they had drafted during those
long hot months in Philadelphia, the venerable
Dr. Franklin arose and "looking toward the
president's chair, at the back of which a rising
sun happened to be painted, observed that
painters had found it difficult to distinguish in
their art between a rising and a setting sun. 'I
have often and often,' said he, 'in the course of
the session and the vicissitudes of my hopes
and fears as to its issue looked at that behind
the presidency, without being able to tell
whether it was rising or setting. Now at length
I have the happiness to know that it is a rising
and not a setting sun.'" [6]

Having come through the Watergate trial of our
constitutional system, we can have more confidence

today that America's future is indeed a rising and
not a setting sun. Confidence in ourselves and our
destiny as a nation under God is necessary to our
fullest participation in His purpose for us in the
world. As Kenneth Clark puts it, "Civilisation
requires a modicum of material prosperity—enough
to provide a little leisure. But, far more, it requires
confidence—confidence in the society in which one
lives, belief in its philosophy, belief in its laws, and
confidence in one's own mental powers. The way
in which the stones of the Pont du Gard are laid is
not only a triumph of technical skill, but shows a
vigorous belief in law and discipline. Vigour, energy,
vitality: all the great civilisations—or civilising
epochs—have had a weight of energy behind
them." [7]

Despite the uncertainties of the present period of
inflation/recession, recovery of confidence in our
fundamental system of government lends hope that
we can and will find ways to cope with our situation.
The word of the Lord comes to us, as to a
discouraged people centuries ago, saying:

> Comfort, comfort my people,
>   says your God.
> Speak tenderly to Jerusalem,
>   and cry to her

that her warfare is ended,
    that her iniquity is pardoned,
that she has received from the Lord's hand
    double for all her sins.

. . . .

but they who wait for the Lord shall renew
        their strength,
    they shall mount up with wings like eagles,
they shall run and not be weary,
    they shall walk and not faint.[8]

Second, I believe God is developing a new
humanity in America by calling us to make a
declaration of amnesty: a broad general amnesty
in which all of us will forgive each other for the
divisions and the hostilities of the time which is past.
An amnesty in which we will be willing to let a
spirit of magnanimity sweep through us, clearing
away ancient grudges and hostilities and blowing
upon us the fresh breeze of a common future. There
is a deep-rooted longing today on the part of the
American people to let old grudges die, and to
affirm the commonly shared values we hold together.
What we have in common is deeper than what we
have in conflict. Leadership that emphasizes the
commonwealth, is low key, modest of promise, and
open in style, will find massive response.

A little perspective helps us to see what we've

been going through in the last ten years, and so
maybe to feel a little better about ourselves. A few
years ago James Reston gave an address at Ohio
State University. He started out by quoting these
words of the philosopher Whitehead: "It is the
first step in wisdom to recognize that the major
advances in civilization are processes which all but
wreck the society in which they occur. The art of
free society consists, first, in the maintenance of the
symbolic code, and secondly, in fearlessness of
revision. Those societies which cannot combine
reverence for their symbols with freedom of revision
must ultimately decay either from anarchy or from
the slow atrophy of a life stifled by useless
shadows."

He continued, "This seems to me to be an almost
perfect definition of the American condition today
with all its divisions, strugglings, yearnings,
controversies, dangers, and opportunities. I cannot
remember a time, and I have not read about a time,
save the very beginning of the Republic, when the
American people were grappling with the hard facts
of life as they are now. There is not a human
relationship in the nation today, whether of husband
and wife, parents and children, employer and
employee, teacher and pupil, preacher and parish-
ioner, that is not under the most searching analysis.

Nor is there another country in the world where
the fundamental problems of life are being faced so
squarely."

How to face those problems? "By maintenance
of the symbolic code and fearlessness of revision." [9]

There are, of course, many people on the right
who want to maintain the symbolic code without
fearless revision, and there are many people on the
left who want fearlessly to revise but without
reverence for the past. So God calls us, I believe, on
the right and on the left, the north and the south,
the east and the west and the middle west, to make
a declaration of amnesty towards 1976. To forgive
those who argued on the other side of the issues of
these recent years. And to accept their forgiveness.
Together to develop a new humanity, incorporating
the partial truths that each side saw, achieving a
peace in which the legitimate concerns of each are
protected for the benefit of all.

There are flags of amnesty being raised in our
country today. In an article entitled "The 'New
South' Is No Longer a Slogan; It's a Description"
Jon Nordheimer writes:

Take George Wallace. Ten years ago he
epitomized the fiery-cross-burning white man

of the Old South. He was a popular symbol of the monkeywrench toughness of a common people whose lives were circumscribed by forces over which they had little control and no understanding. In the course of one afternoon recently, the Alabama Governor crowned a black beauty queen at the University of Alabama in Tuscaloosa and then went to Tuskegee to welcome a conference of forty black Southern mayors. Weakened by the wounds from an assassin's bullets, and locked in his wheelchair, the Governor of Alabama that day became a metaphor for change in the white South that had once sought to block both the school house and the court house doors.

The South's black people, for the most part, have had a superabundance of good will in helping the white man on his long voyage out of anger and adjust to the new order of things. It is the kind of patience shown by Representative Andrew Young, Jr., Democrat of Georgia, the first black Congressman from the Deep South in modern times, when he became the only black in the House to vote to confirm Gerald Ford for Vice President, despite Mr. Ford's opposition to certain civil rights legislation in the past.

"Out of my own southern experience I have confidence that people can overcome past parochial views and develop a broader

perspective that takes into account the interest of all people," said the former aide to the late Dr. King. "Decent men placed in positions of trust will serve decently." [10]

There is magnanimity of spirit! There is a desire not to lock a man into the prejudices of the past but to encourage the broadest, most generous portions of his spirit for the future. It is ironic that Boston, the cradle of American liberty, should be torn by racial strife in the period of the Bicentennial. The conflict there of ethnic, metropolitan and racial values is a bitter reminder of the complexity of achieving justice in every city and town of our nation. Even so, the flag of racial amnesty is aloft in the land.

President Ford tried to send up another flag of amnesty when he called on Americans to be lenient toward those who resisted participation in the Vietnam war, and offered them a process of reconciliation. It is significant that former Defense Secretary Melvin R. Laird and Army Secretary Robert F. Froelke both felt, while still in those offices, that an amnesty plan for draft dodgers, deserters and others who resisted the draft should eventually be implemented. A reporter quoted Laird as saying, "We have always felt in this country that justice must be administered with compassion and mercy."

The call for amnesty or reconciliation on the part of responsible moderate leaders is a reflection of our growing recognition that we all made mistakes in those Vietnam years. Some of us supported that war for years because we thought it was the right thing to do. Others of us, in various ways, resisted that war for years because we felt it was the right thing to do.

All of us bear some responsibility for our nation's behavior in those years. And therefore all of us need both to forgive and to be forgiven. Perhaps the testimony of Retired Army Colonel David Hackworth represents a change in attitude with which

many of us can in some degree identify. While our
government has proceeded with a conditional
amnesty plan which has not been completely
successful, the spirit of Hackworth's vision tugs at
all our hearts. He is one of the nation's most
decorated combat soldiers, having received more
than one hundred American and foreign decorations
for his exploits in the Korean and Vietnam wars.
He spent five years in Vietnam combat assign-
ments. He writes:

> The number of young men who resisted the
> war in Viet Nam is without parallel in American
> history. There were approximately 400,000
> incidents of desertion during the long course of
> the war. Some 28,000 deserters are still fugitives
> —2,100 of them living abroad.
> And there were some 5,000 convictions for
> draft violations. Some 70,000 resisters—
> including the 28,000 deserters—have not yet
> been dealt with.
> In addition, there are thousands of men who
> received less than honorable discharges because
> they refused to support the war.
> I now believe that the majority of these
> young men resisted the war because of
> conscience.
> This had not always been my view. Back

in the days when I thought our cause was right, our leaders honest, and that the war was in line with American tradition and the country's best interests, I could not understand how anyone could refuse to serve his country.

But much has happened since then.

All of those events have led to a change in my viewpoint. I now find myself in the ironic position of defending those kids whom I considered long-haired gutless freaks, who fled when their country called upon them.

They were right. I was wrong. They are the real conscience of our land, and should not be forced to hide or suffer further punishment.

They saw that the war was bad, long before most of us. Their outcry served as a spearhead that contributed to the public outrage which finally caused our reluctant government to disentangle our nation from the quagmire of Viet Nam. Their only crime was to clearly see that we were wrong—ahead of the rest of us. Their finding was premature.

What makes the matter difficult is that not all who resisted are pure conscientious objectors. Like so many bad apples hiding among good in a barrel, there are those posing as resisters who were motivated not by principle but rather fear and selfishness.

But who can play God to determine the "good" ones from the "bad" ones?

Those who resisted could have taken another route, which millions of young Americans took. They knew about college and teaching deferments, and reserve and national guard havens and about the "right" doctor who could provide a medical deferment.

They were aware of the fact that if one had power, contacts, and money, there were many possibilities; anything was possible, for they had seen too many famous athletes, celebrities, and sons of important people who were awarded legal "resister" status. . . .

After agonizing over this problem for three years, I believe unconditional amnesty is the right answer for a wrong war. Let there be no strings attached. Give amnesty to everyone. The good conscientious objectors and the phony conscientious objectors.

Give it to Lt. William Calley, a convicted murderer, an obscenity who blackened the name of the Army and indelibly stained the honor of the country. But give him amnesty so we can get on with the task of finding internal peace.

Free everyone who resisted. Open the prison doors and take down the barriers of our borders. Recall the bad discharges and give those who refused to support the war an honorable discharge. Allow everyone to contribute to our society rather than assigning less-than-human

status to them. We must stop the punishment
and start the forgetting.

Let us stop the bitter recrimination, dis-
sension, and division. Let us stop looking for
someone to blame for our actions in Viet Nam
and start looking for some method of healing
and reconciliation for our nation.

We have suffered enough for it, and those
who refused to serve have not gone unpunished.
Let us forgive.[11]

Let us indeed forgive and forget, and accept
forgiveness, "with malice toward none and charity
for all."

In addition to Lincoln's words, two of the most
memorable biblical passages taught me as a child
come to my mind as pertinent. The author of Psalm
103 wrote:

> The Lord is merciful and gracious,
>   slow to anger and abounding in
>   steadfast love.
>
> . . . .
>
> He does not deal with us according
>   to our sins,
>   nor requite us according to our
>   iniquities.
> For as the heavens are high above
>   the earth,

> so great is his steadfast love to-
> ward those who fear him;
> as far as the east is from the west,
> so far does he remove our trans-
> gressions from us.[12]

May the removal of transgressions abound
among us!

Jesus said; "And forgive us our debts, As we also
have forgiven our debtors. . . . For if you forgive
men their trespasses, your heavenly Father also
will forgive you; but if you do not forgive men their
trespasses, neither will your Father forgive your
trespasses." [13]

Forgiveness is a two-way street. Unconditional
amnesty in human relations is the Lord's idea.

Second, then, I believe God is developing a new
humanity in America by calling us to make a
declaration of amnesty.

Third, I believe God is developing a new humanity
in America by calling us to see ourselves real.
Seeing ourselves real is not a matter of pounding
our chests and shouting, "We're the best!"; nor is
it a matter of beating our breasts and moaning,
"We are the worst!"

In the last ten years we have lost our innocence.
Assassinations, Vietnam, Watergate, the energy

crisis, inflation and recession have made us painfully
aware that we are not immune from the tragedies
and failures that beset other nations. Power and
innocence often go together in a person or in a
nation. Our power has made it easy for us to think
that we are more virtuous, more compassionate,
more unselfish than people in other nations. How
could so powerful and prosperous a nation be wrong?
As the Arab nations' oil power confronts and limits
our own power, we are reminded that it is char-
acteristic of the Lord of history, on occasion, to use
the power of one nation to curb the power of
another.[14]

In a discussion group recently the question was
raised, "Is the average American more compassionate than the average Chinese, or African, or
Norwegian, or Finn?" There was silence for a bit,
and then a general recognition that God's human
material is much the same everywhere. People
love their children. People love their country. People
do what they think is best, in the best way that
they can.

It may now be easier for other nations to live
with us. And we may have an easier time living
with ourselves. We don't have such a myth of
innocence and virtue to live up to any longer. We

know in the post-Vietnam era that every nation operates primarily on the basis of what it regards as its self-interest. America does. Every nation makes mistakes. America does. Every nation has a unique contribution to make to the peace and health of the world. America does, and in spades. A healthy reevaluation of what success means for America in the decade ahead may find us more concerned with human values and with the development of a more just and compassionate society. If pride goes before a fall, humility may go before a getting up again.

Because we have lost our innocence, it may now be possible for us to gain wisdom, a wisdom born out of failure, tempered by magnanimity, and nourished by our noblest roots. Anthony Lewis wrote on July 5, 1973:

> Someone once proposed to Thomas Jefferson a celebration of his birthday. "The only birthday which I recognize," he said, "is that of my country's liberties." It is a good time now, if a little painful, to think about Jefferson. He was such an extraordinary embodiment of the qualities that once characterized the leaders of the U. S. and made possible our independence. He disdained wealth and show, respected learning, and had faith in the ultimate power

94

of reason, if left unfettered by myth or privilege.
Remembering George III, he was against the
glorification of Presidents. Before the Constitution or the Bill of Rights existed, he said
that if we had to choose "whether we should
have a government without newspapers, or
newspapers without government, I should not
hesitate to prefer the latter." As President, he
suffered attacks from the press as caustic as
anything imaginable today. He minded and
he had a temper but he never weakened in his
commitment to freedom of speech—not even
for those in the most profound disagreement
with his premises.

He said in his first inaugural address in 1801,
"If there be any among us who would wish to
dissolve this union, or to change its republican
form, let them stand undisturbed as monuments
of the safety with which error of opinion may
be tolerated where reason is left free to combat
it." [That's confidence in freedom and liberty,
isn't it!]

. . . He was not a man who depended upon
political power for his satisfaction. He had
inner resources. He was a scientist, an architect
of real distinction, a scholar. He valued his part
in the founding of the University of Virginia
as much or more than being President. Nor did
he grow rich from office. "When a man assumes

a public trust," he wrote, "he should consider
himself as public property." He spent his last
years at the edge of poverty facing the possibility
of having to sell his beloved house, Monticello.
And even then, he refused assistance from the
state.

He was a revolutionary, but of a peculiarly
American, old-fashioned kind. The revolution
that he and his colleagues declared on July 4,
1776, was one in favor of law. It was on their
very ground that the King had violated the
unwritten Constitution—the understandings of
the lawful society. The Declaration of
Independence complains of George's
usurpations.

Jefferson wrote to John Adams regularly
and theirs was a remarkable correspondence.
They were the deepest political opponents,
rivals for the Presidency in 1800, spokesmen
for conflicting regions and governmental
philosophies. But those differences did not lead
them to doubt each other's honor or patriotism.
In their retirement, they corresponded regularly
—Jefferson from Monticello, and Adams from
home in Quincy, Massachusetts. They would
speculate about Calvinism, the proper trans-
lation of Greek phrases, world affairs, the
ominous significance of slavery. On July 4,
1826, when Jefferson was 83, just after noon,
he died at Monticello. A few hours later in

Quincy, not knowing of his friend's death, John Adams died. His last words were "Jefferson still survives." [15]

And he was right. The spirit of Jefferson and Adams still survives among us today. We are ripe to graduate from a preoccupation with ideology right or left and to take our politics with a bit more humility and humor. We are both judged by the faith of our founding fathers and nourished by it. To see ourselves real as a nation is to admit our failures and to acknowledge our noblest potential as the nation presently most able under God to foster on this earth the development of a new humanity.

Our Bicentennial year is upon us. Could we celebrate our independence by committing ourselves to the development of a new humanity in this nation, a new humanity energized by a recovery of confidence in ourselves, tempered by seeing ourselves real, and enabled by declaring amnesty for all our people? Could we celebrate our independence by making a declaration of interdependence —the interdependence of all nations in which there is safety and dignity for each, in which the only peace with honor will be a peace without victory,

a peace without the humiliation of the weak, but
with the restraint of the strong?

The end of the American future, the death in
mid-life of our narcissistic self-image, could signal
the development of a new humanity in this land,
and progress toward completion of the unfinished
revolution that began two centuries ago. Let
churches and synagogues in every town and city,
together with other institutions and citizens,
encourage the total community to use this period of
time for a profound spiritual and ethical evaluation
of our national goals. Let the people of this and
every nation join the Lord of history in developing
a single new humanity on the face of the earth.

    The people will live on.
The learning and blundering people will live on.
    They will be tricked and sold and again sold
And go back to the nourishing earth for rootholds,
    The people so peculiar in renewal and comeback,
    You can't laugh off their capacity to take it. . . .

This old anvil—the people, yes—
This old anvil laughs at many broken hammers.
    There are men who can't be bought.
    There are women beyond purchase.
    The fireborn are at home in fire.
    The stars make no noise.

98

You can't hinder the wind from blowing.
Time is a great teacher.
Who can live without hope?

In the darkness with a great bundle of grief
    the people march.
In the night, and overhead a shovel of stars for
    keeps, the people march:
            "Where to? what next?
            Where to? what next?" [16]

In the first three chapters we have explored what
it means to be a successful person, congregation
and nation. Now in the three remaining chapters
we will explore what it means to be a successful
Christian. Far from exhaustive, my thoughts are
only suggestive as to what may be involved in being
a "successful"—that is, real and effective—
Christian. Use whatever is useful to you in your
own life, and find whatever fresh meaning you can
in your own struggle to live as one of God's losers,
winners, and wounded healers.

Chapter 4

What does it mean to be a

successful Christian?

GOD'S LOSERS

Charlie Brown made an important observation on winning and losing while talking one day to Lucy. He said, "I feel bad when I lose. But when I win, I feel so guilty!" We're hung up on winning and losing, aren't we? I mean, if Charlie Brown is worried about it, we're all worried about it!

Vince Lombardi, the late great coach of the

103

Green Bay Packers, once said, "Winning isn't everything. Winning is the only thing." Is it really? A part of the common culture now is the slogan, "Show me a good loser, and I'll show you a loser." Is it bad to be a good loser?

In *Sports Illustrated* two years ago, I was delighted to see a prayer written by a friend and former college classmate of mine, Sid Lovett. The prayer was given on the occasion of the Annual Kodak Banquet and Award for the Coach of the Year of the American Football Coaches' Association. Part of Sid Lovett's prayer reads: "Thou art a God of mercy and so we lift before Thy care those coaches, who with endurance and honor but a losing record, are grateful for a new year. Deliver them from the nightmares of instant replay and sullen alumni. And if it please Thee, bestow upon them sure-fingered ends, fleet runners with secure cartilages, and linemen of granite." [1]

This is a prayer for losers—coaches who didn't win the big ones, kids who didn't get all A's or make the first team, or get the girl or guy they really wanted, parents and kids who drive each other up the wall, husbands and wives who are barely making it or failed to make it, anybody who gets kicked in the stomach with bad news. It's a prayer for people like you and me whenever we experience the loss of something or someone important or precious to us. Is there any one of us who hasn't lost something important lately? Don't we all know something about losing in some areas of our lives?

We say so quickly, "She's a winner," or, "He's a loser." But we know from our own experience that to be human means to win some of the struggles in our lives and to lose some. Sometimes on the outside it looks like we're winning, while we know on the inside we're losing. And yet sometimes we see people in circumstances of pain and loss who look as though they think they're winning something important.

William Blake puts it the way it is:

> Man was made for Joy and Woe;
> And when this we rightly know,
> Thro' the World we safely go,
> Joy and woe are woven fine,
> A clothing for the soul divine.

Let me put it in my own words:

> Winning and losing are woven rough
> To make our humanity tender/tough.

Jesus lost it all. That parade of the palms was the beginning of the end. The opposition had been

105

gathering and closing in. His options narrowed.
Either he had to withdraw from his public ministry
and enter into permanent hiding, or he had to risk
everything in a final appeal to the nation in
Jerusalem. He chose to go for broke in Jerusalem
with maximum exposure.

Jesus lost it all for the love of God and man. What
might it mean for you and me, with Jesus, to be
God's losers?

First, life makes losers of us all. To lose,
fundamentally, is not to be in control of what is
vitally important to you. It's to run into walls that
don't move. It's to fall over cliffs that you didn't
build and didn't see. It's to learn that there are no
guarantees. It's to experience limitation, to suffer
transience, to become vulnerable.

Jesus couldn't control the events that finally
swamped him. From the very beginning he tasted
failure. He was rejected by his hometown
congregation and even thrown out of the synagogue.
His family thought he was some religious fanatic.
His closest friends, even at the end, misunderstood
his mission and betrayed, denied, and deserted him.
The nation wouldn't accept him. And at the last,
he felt forsaken even by God. He knew what it was
to lose everything.

We can't control the events that finally swamp us either. Early or late, we all lose control and become vulnerable.

A man in his early fifties experiences a change of regimes at work. Some older people on the job are given early retirement, new young men are brought in to make the future. He's not old enough to retire, but he's too old to fit in with these young tigers. All his life he's been a winner. Suddenly he's losing— losing out. How fragile our security is and how tied into the institutions we serve is our dignity.

Some years ago when I lived in Columbus and was minister at First Community Church, I was flying home. A member of our congregation was on the same plane. His wife met him at the airport with their two little boys, and he introduced me to his sons. One of the boys said to him, "Is that the Mr. Raines that owns First Community Church?" I wasn't swift enough to reply, "Young man, you have it almost right. I am the Mr. Raines that First Community Church owns."

Institutions and systems own big chunks of us— don't they?—for better and for worse. People own chunks of our lives and the more important they are to us, the more vulnerable we are to them.

Parents may be successful in business, beautiful

in appearance, rich in friendship, and raise their children the best way they know how. Yet one of their children rebels, maybe for very good reasons, grows hostile and distant, swings out into some strange unconventional orbit, and doesn't want to communicate. Suddenly, we who have been winners in everything else discover we're losing where it matters the most to us.

Or take the All-American couple—riding high. The marriage grows sour and stale. They begin to learn how to avoid spending time alone together. They are winning everywhere else but losing together.

Or you have a routine physical examination. The doctor tells you that you've got cancer, and within a week you know that you've got less than a year.

None of us is immune to losing. No one escapes the experience of loss.

> Winning and losing are woven rough
> To make our humanity tender/tough.

First, life makes losers of us all. But second, we can choose to be God's losers. We can't control what happens to us, but we can decide how we will respond to what happens to us.

Jesus chose to go to Jerusalem. He did not withdraw. He didn't go into hiding. He did not abdicate his mission. He chose to risk it all for the sake of living out of his deepest integrity. He chose to go with God's leading, though he didn't know where it would lead him. He couldn't be sure what would happen. He had no guarantees. He couldn't see around any corners. He embraced his vulnerability for the love of God and man.

You and I also are free to choose to go to our Jerusalems, whatever they are. We can embrace our own vulnerability wherever and in whatever ways we are vulnerable. We can choose to live out of our deepest knowing and being, accepting losses and facing pain for the sake of what matters most to us.

A woman said to me years ago, "I faced the question of staying with my husband or getting a divorce. I decided to stay. It's not been easy for either of us. But I'm sticking with him, and we're making the best that we can together." She has chosen and is choosing to be one of God's losers, accepting with her eyes wide open the severe limitations of her context and her life, eating the losses, making the most out of the least and the best out of the worst.

We can share our experiences of loss together in

ways that are appropriate and useful. We can
acknowledge to ourselves and to others that we don't
have it made, that we're hurting. I received a letter
recently that read in part: "One minute I'm on
top, and the next I'm muddling again. One minute
our marriage is secure and passionate; the next it is
a step away from disaster. One minute I'm really
sure; so soon again unsure. But it's good to know
that we're all struggling together."

I think when we lose something or someone
precious and important to us, we learn what we can

learn in no other way. We learn that it's OK to
lose. To be human is to lose sometimes, in some
things, with some people.

Only when we ourselves have failed in some way
are we able truly to sympathize with other people
in their failures. Only when we ourselves experience
humiliation, whether private or public, can we
understand the feelings of others who are humiliated.
Only when we realize our own desperate need to be
forgiven by someone we've hurt are we able to
forgive someone who hurts us. Only when we begin
to understand the ways in which our power,
whatever it is, has in part corrupted us, corroded
our compassion and blinded our vision, do we begin
to understand the mixed motivations we see in
other people, and the mixture of good and evil in
every human action. Only when we lose our own
innocence do we gain the wisdom to know that there
are no good guys and bad guys, but only people
who do some good things and some bad things, and
some things that are very mixed in their results.

We can share our experience of loss. And, more
than that, we can even celebrate our losing as well
as our winning. A couple shared with a few friends
an experience of celebrating losing they participated
in recently. A young friend of theirs had cancer.

Many of the friends of this young person were
concerned, and wanted to reach out to her together.
One Sunday more than eighty of them met in a
little church to pray for her in the hospital. Her
husband and two of her children were there in the
church. There were many expressions of prayer, and
there were many tears. And then this young
husband got up and said, "Let's not have any more
crying. This thing hasn't licked Doris yet, and if it
does, we have Jesus and the love of God." So they
celebrated there in that little church the life of their
friend facing death, and they shared, through their
tears, the love of God.

Every Sunday worship is meant to be a celebration
like that, where we can offer our losses as well as
our gains, where we can face the worst of which we
are presently afraid and offer it and ourselves to the
Lord of life and death.

Every day prayer is meant to be a celebration
like that where we can go down into whatever is
the deepest darkness we know in search of a light
that can shine in that darkness. Every moment, even
this one, we can consciously embrace our most
frightening vulnerability in search of the power
within us that will enable us to cope no matter
what.

James Reston gave a eulogy at the funeral of his friend and colleague, Orvil Dryfoos. He said:

> The death of Orvil Dryfoos was blamed on heart failure, but that obviously could not have been the reason. Orv's heart never failed him or anybody else. Ask the reporters on the Times. It was as steady as the stars. Ask anybody in the company of his friends. It was as faithful as the tides. Ask his beloved wife and family. No matter what the doctors say, they cannot blame his heart. In the spiritual sense, his heart was not a failure but his greatest success. He had room in it for every joy and for everybody else's joy. This was the thing that set him apart—this warmness and openness and purity of spirit. This considerateness—of his mother whom he telephoned every day, of his wife and family, of his colleagues and his friends.
>
> And this uncorrupted heart, broken or no, is what is likely to be remembered about him. Let us then honor Orvil Dryfoos with grateful remembrance and celebration more than tears —for we will never be able to cry as much as he has made us laugh.[3]

Let us then honor Jesus with grateful remembrance and celebration more than tears for we will never be able to cry as much as he has made us laugh. And let us honor each other and ourselves with celebration, for we are God's losers, learning how to laugh through our tears.

P.S. I wrote a note of appreciation to my friend, Sid Lovett, for his prayer for losers, and he wrote back, "We still believe that God turns losers into winners. So keep smarting, as well as smiling."

Chapter 5

What does it mean to be a

successful Christian?

GOD'S WINNERS

One Maundy Thursday evening I was sitting in the sanctuary of First Community Church during the communion service, listening to the beautiful music being sung by the choir. As I watched and listened to the deacons as one by one they came up to read the Scripture, something blipped in my heart. I felt for a moment that I was seeing each

man real. I knew each face, I knew each person.
I felt close to each man.

I had a feeling of compassion and love for our
whole congregation. I remembered words that a
Roman Catholic priest, Georges Bernanos, had
written one time about his parish: "My parish! The
words can't even be spoken without a kind of
soaring love. . . . But if only the good God would
open my eyes and unseal my ears, so that I might
behold the face of my parish and hear its voice. . . .
The face of my parish! The look in the eyes. . . .
They must be gentle, suffering patient eyes. I feel
they must be rather like mine when I cease struggling
and let myself be borne along in the great invisible
flux that sweeps us all, helter-skelter, the living and
the dead, into the deep waters of Eternity. And
those would be the eyes of all Christianity, of all
parishes—perhaps of the poor human race itself.
Our Lord saw them from the Cross. 'Forgive them
for they know not what they do.' " [1]

The face of our parish—your face—my face. What
does the Lord see as he reads between the lines in
our faces? A yearning that soars beyond what is
now possible, a sorrow that sits deep in the soul, an
ache that comes and goes and comes back again, a
human ache that reaches through today's illness,

divorce, fear, frustration, terror, whatever the
darkness. Faces that have lost much, yet hope for
still more. Faces brave and beautiful. Your face—
my face—the face of the human race itself.

Later that Maundy Thursday evening I was
putting my six-year-old son, Bobby, to bed. We had
been to the family communion service earlier and
had heard this word "Maundy." He asked me to tell
him again what Maundy Thursday meant. I told
him it was the last time Jesus had supper with his
friends, and that Good Friday was the day he was
killed, and Easter was the most wonderful day of
the year because that was the day when God
raised Jesus from the dead.

Bobby looked at me with those boy-blue eyes and
said, "Daddy, will Easter ever happen to me?" I
said, "Yes, I believe it will." And he said, "No, it
won't. Jesus was special. He was Jesus Christ
Superstar." I laughed and said, "You're special,
too. You're Bobby Super Boy." And so we laughed
together and I rubbed his back some more and he
went to sleep. We had our little Easter there
together.

I realized, later, that his question is our question
too. Will Easter ever happen to me? Jesus was
special, and so were Paul and Peter. So are some

119

people we know today who have remarkable
changes and rebirths in their lives. But will Easter
ever happen to me?

The good news is that Easter is happening to you
and to me right now. Despite our losses, our deaths
and disappointments, the little deaths and the big
ones, we are all winners—God's winners—because
of what God did on that first Easter and continues
to do today. We call what happened on that first
Easter the resurrection of Jesus. How Jesus was
raised from the dead is a fascinating mystery to
which I can find no thoroughly satisfying rational
explanation.

But, much more important, the demonstrable
fact is that the friends of Jesus had far more power
and light after his death than they did before. The
Easter event did not give them a new lease on life:
it gave them a lease on a new life. And Easter
happens to us, as it did to them, when we discover
in our own experience that no matter what darkness
we are in, a light is shining there. And nothing can
put it out. Nothing can separate you or me from
the love of God—nothing at all.

That takes more than believing. It takes experiencing firsthand. Where is the evidence that Easter
is real, that Easter is happening to you and me

now today? I think it's all around, shining in the
lines on our faces, if we have eyes to see. Easter is
primarily a matter of recognition. In most of the
Easter stories Jesus appears first as a stranger—on
the beach, in the garden, in the upper room, on the
road to Emmaus. Then, a moment later, he is
recognized; he is seen real. So Easter happens to us
when we recognize the love of God happening in
our very lives.

Easter has been happening to Bob Schatzman.
Bob was born and bred a Jew. He grew up in
an atmosphere in his home where he felt unloved
and unable to express his feelings. He got into serious
trouble and was in prison for many years. In the
last few years, he came to know some of the people
in the First Community Church prison concern
group. He participated in many of the activities
of the life of First Community Church. When he was
released from prison, he went to live with George
and Linda Norris, members of the congregation.

After over a year of participating in the life of
the church, he came up to me one Sunday and said,
"Bob, I'm thinking about joining the church. But
you know, as a Jew, accepting Christ is difficult
for me, and I've learned in my particular experience
to be very wary and skeptical. I'm not sure I

believe in God. But I sure believe in the people in
this church!"

I said to him, "The first thing is not to believe in
God; it's to try to start loving God with all your
heart. And if you're comfortable with trying to do
that, then come and join us." So he did. In the
months that followed, he shared in and enriched
the life of the congregation. Then one day he said
to me, "Bob, I want you to know something. I tried
loving God with all my heart as you suggested.
And in the last several months here with my special
friends, I know I have experienced the love of God.
I find that I'm now able to believe in God because
I've experienced his love here." Have you, too, in
some way experienced the love of God in the
fellowship of your church or with a few of your
friends? Is Easter also happening in you, too, and
in me, a little?

Easter began happening in the lives of many older
people at First Community Church in recent years.
One morning I sat in on a meeting of the senior
forum, which is a group assisting Nancy Heath in
her ministry to older people. Some good ideas were
expressed. There was some joshing and joking.
Haydn Evans even sang a Welsh song for us! And
at one point we laughed so loudly I wondered if

other people in the building would wonder who that raucous crowd of people in the library might be!

Nancy arranged rides to church for a few of our older people who had trouble getting there. And one of them said proudly to her one Sunday, "I was brought to church today by a deacon, no less!"

Nancy writes: "To walk in on a lonely woman just as she is facing the imminent death of her husband, to sponge the face of a dying woman, to share a problem and perhaps lend some hope, and to see their faces light up when next we meet

and I call them by name, gives meaning to this
work that transcends all the nitty-gritty. To see
the pattern of awareness and caring that is evolving
and spreading is exciting." It is exciting to watch
people being blessed or touched in some way. Is
Easter also happening in you?

Easter is happening in people who are facing an
uncertain future. Some time ago a woman talked
with me about a friend who had cancer. She
wondered how to relate to this friend, how to talk
to her, how open and real and honest to be and
so on. We talked about those things, and then a
few months later a letter came from this woman in
which she said, "My friend with cancer is better
right now. She is not only stronger, she is incredibly
beautiful. I love the moments we have together.
We seem to nourish each other. A strong and realistic
relationship like this makes me aware of *now*
and how fantastic it is. I'm grateful for many *now*
relationships and moments in my life."

Are there some now relationships and moments
in our lives in the face of an uncertain future?
Moments which make us aware how fantastic *now*
is? What beauty and joy can we taste today that no
tomorrow can destroy? Can Easter power and light
give us victories over transience and enable us to

enjoy with all our hearts today what cannot be
held for sure tomorrow?

Easter is happening in the life of a friend of mine,
a businessman. He told me about the tough year
he's gone through. He's branch manager of a national
corporation. He's always been a winner—successful,
competent, hard working. Things have gone well
for him, as they should, because he did well. But
over a few months, all of a sudden, two or three
bad mistakes in judgment by men on his staff had
brought his part of the firm into serious financial
jeopardy. He spent sleepless nights and seven-day
work weeks trying to turn that situation around.

Finally he felt he had no alternative but to tell
the president and owner of the company just
how serious things were. And so he called him
on the phone and said, "I've got some bad news
and it's serious. I want to talk with you about it
personally." So he flew to the city where his boss
lived and they met in his office. My friend said to
me, "It was hard, but I laid out the bad news. I
was afraid because I didn't know what was going
to come."

His boss listened and then said, "Sam, I'm so
glad it's just a business problem. I've been afraid
it was your health. Now let's see what we can do to

improve the financial situation." As my friend was
telling me this, tears came to his eyes and his voice
choked up. He said, "What a great man, my
boss!" Yes, great in kindness and in putting
persons before problems.

God's love is unconditionally kind. We get fleeting
glimpses of it now and then as my friend did in the
concern of his boss. Only God's love is for always
and it can always be counted on. There's no
doubt about it. We need have no fear at all. No
matter what is done to us or what we do, God's
love is right there with us and for us one hundred
percent.

Is Easter also happening in you through
someone's kind concern? Or are you passing Easter
along in your kind concern for someone else
looking to you in fear and in hope?

Easter has been happening to me and a friend of
mine. Ted Loder and I worked together in a
co-ministry for eight years in Philadelphia. It
was a hard structure to work in. It poised two
people to compete with each other in ways that
were destructive as well as creative. It was abrasive.
It often stifled the warm feelings that we had for
each other. When I left Philadelphia many years
ago, our relationship was at a courteous but cool

standstill. In the years since then our friendship
has been free to flower and to grow in ways it
never could while we worked together in that
structure. I went back to preach for Ted at his
request a few years ago at a time when the
congregation was wounded. I shared some of my
own wounds with the congregation, including
an experience of loneliness I shared with my
six-year-old son one night while skipping rocks on
a Lake Michigan beach. Healing comfort seemed to
flow for many of us. The next week there came a
beautiful letter from Ted during the course of
which he wrote: "I find myself with the child's
wish that what has happened since we separated
could have happened before. That somehow we
could go back and do it over. Not erasing the good
things—and they were many—but adding something
to it beautiful that got lost or that we prevented
from happening. But that impossibility is a part
of those wounds you mentioned—right? You are
a friend and I am more than grateful for that.
Maybe some day, in some way, I will be able to
repay some part of what I owe you. Maybe it
will be finding just a good flat rock for you to
skip on Lake Michigan. And it will keep on skipping
so long as it will make you laugh."

Is there some relationship which has been broken
or changed or is hurting in which you can feel
Easter beginning to happen, or at least its possibility?
Is it possible somehow to laugh through our tears?
We can't redo yesterday. We know that. We don't
need to. Easter somehow makes it possible to
gather up all of yesterday's sorrow and hurt, and
suffer it to deepen, enrich and enlarge our humanity
today.

Pierre Teilhard put it: "Like an artist making
use of a fault or an impurity in the stone he is
sculpting or the bronze he is casting, so as to produce
more exquisite lines or a more beautiful tone, God,
without sparing us the partial deaths, nor the final
death, which form an essential part of our lives,
transfigures them by integrating them in a better
plan—provided we trust lovingly in Him." [2] A
human work of art that stands free and real,
brave and beautiful in the face of death.

It has taken me a long time, forty-eight years,
to begin to understand that winning is not avoiding
losing, but rather accepting my losses, acknowledging
my failures and experiencing my partial deaths; and
while doing so, knowing a love operating within
me and for me that can accept and transform all
the partial deaths. Being God's winners doesn't

wipe out our losses nor erase painful memories, but enables us to trust in grace for a healing of memories and a regeneration of hope. Though wounded, we can yet be healers. Indeed, the truth may be that only through wounds does the healing power flow, and only the wounded can be God's healers.

Chapter 6

What does it mean to be a

successful Christian?

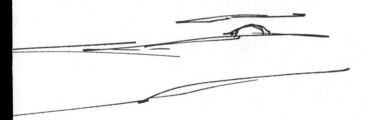

GOD'S WOUNDED HEALERS

One night perhaps ten years ago, in a group conversation a man shared his personal pilgrimage of struggle and suffering. He concluded with a comment that I have remembered ever since: "I am one of the walking wounded." I wasn't conscious then of my own inner ache. But today I understand that I, too, am one of the walking

wounded. Are you also in the ranks of the
walking wounded?

Somewhere Kazantzakis says, "Every woman
has a wound that will not heal." And so does every
man. Henri Nouwen in his book *The Wounded
Healer* suggests that loneliness may be the most
painful wound in the human heart. He writes: "The
wound of loneliness is like the Grand Canyon—a
deep incision in the surface of our existence which
has become an inexhaustible source of beauty and
self-understanding." [1]

For the first forty years of my life I thought
that I wasn't lonely, and tried to escape it or deny
it by much talk or activity. Only in recent years
have I begun to discover that I am much less
gregarious than I thought I was, more of a private
person. I have come to understand that it isn't
weakness to acknowledge our needs, to confess
that we are lonely, and that it is not healthy for us
to anesthetize our wounds to escape or avoid the
pain. To be human is to be wounded with loneliness.
Nouwen writes with a clear wisdom:

> When we are impatient, when we want to
> give up our loneliness and try to overcome the
> separation and the incompleteness we feel, too
> soon, we easily relate to our human world with

132

devastating expectations. We ignore what we already know with the deep-seated, intuitive knowledge that no love or friendship, no intimate embrace or tender kiss, no community, commune or collective, no man or woman, will ever be able to satisfy our desire to be released from our lonely condition. This truth is so disconcerting and painful that we are more prone to play games with our fantasies than to face the truth of our existence. Thus we keep hoping that one day we will find the man who really understands our experiences, the woman who will bring peace to our restless life, the job where we can fulfill our potentials, the book which will explain everything, and the place where we can feel at home. Such false hope leads us to make exhausting demands and prepares us for bitterness and dangerous hostility when we start discovering that nobody, and nothing, can live up to our absolutistic expectations.

Many marriages are ruined because neither partner was able to fulfill the often hidden hope that the other would take away his or her loneliness. And many celibates, voluntary or involuntary, live with the naive dream that in the intimacy of marriage their loneliness will be taken away.[2]

Our loneliness takes us by surprise. One evening

a few years ago my six-year-old son, Bob, and I
were standing on the beach of Lake Michigan. It
was sunset in July. It was one of those moments
when I looked out over the water till it touched the
horizon lit by the setting sun. I was pensive and
felt my tininess against the darkening sky and the
transience of my life's time with Bob. He was
skipping rocks. He looked up at me, saw my face,
and said, "Daddy, are you lonely?" I looked down
at him and nodded. He dropped his rock, reached
over and hugged my leg. We two stood there
for a moment, looking out over the water. My son
comforted me.

The cry of the walking wounded—your cry and
mine—was sounded by Jeremiah calling out of his
own wounds. "My grief is beyond healing, my
heart is sick within me. . . . For the wound of the
daughter of my people is my heart wounded. . . .
Is there no balm in Gilead? Is there no physician
there?" [3] Christianity gives a simple yes to that
question. There is a physician there—and here.
There is a balm in Gilead. All Christianity comes to
focus in a man on a cross. This is what Paul meant
when he wrote to the Corinthians, "When I came
to you, my brothers . . . I did not use long words
and great learning. For I made up my mind to
forget everything while I was with you except

Jesus Christ, and especially his death on the cross." [4]
Jesus Christ nailed to the cross is the balm in Gilead,
Columbus, New York, and where you may live. He
is the wounded healer from whose wounds healing
power flows into our wounded lives.

The poet Roethke writes:

Mist alters the rocks. What can I tell my bones?
My desire's a wind trapped in a cave.
The spirit declares itself to these rocks.
I'm a small stone, loose in the shale.
Love is my wound. [5]

Love is *my* wound. Love is *your* wound. As
Roethke puts it, "Love is not love until love's
vulnerable." [6]

Jesus Christ nailed to the cross is the love of God
made vulnerable, visible, and available to you and
me. It is important to me that Jesus was lonely.
It makes him more real to me and gives me
confidence that he understands me in my
loneliness. "Foxes have holes, and birds of the air
have nests; but the Son of man has nowhere to lay
his head." [7] No home, no wife, no children.
Nobody knows the trouble we've seen. Nobody
knows but Jesus. But he knows; he knows.
And he makes it believable to us that God
knows and cares. As we lay bare our wounds

135

before the wounded healer, we make the strange
discovery that our wounds are a primary source
of self-understanding. Nouwen writes: "perhaps
the painful awareness of loneliness is an invitation
to transcend our limitations and look beyond the
boundaries of our existence. The awareness of
loneliness might be a gift we must protect and guard,
because our loneliness reveals to us an inner empti-
ness that can be destructive when misunderstood,
but filled with promise for him who can tolerate
its sweet pain." [8]

Our wounds are a primary source of
self-understanding, but they are also a vehicle
of self-revelation to other people. They are a
primary connection with the vital humanity of
another. I was raised, as maybe you were, to hide
my wounds, to cover my grief and pain: "Big
boys don't cry." And so I restrained my tears, until
one night a few years ago in an encounter group,
I found myself shaking with sobs, crying out
tears that had been in there for a long time. Another
man next to me began to heave with his own
sobbing, and at the time I thought he was feeling
sorry for me. Later he told me that my pain had
triggered his own inner pain which had nothing to
do with me and that he was crying out of his own

wounds. Many times since then I've experienced
the fact of one person's suffering connecting with
another's through all kinds of barriers and defenses.
Our wounds are the visa into the country of another
person's deep being. They are the badge of our
own humanity, a sign that love is our wound, love
made vulnerable. Have you found your wounds
to be a human bridge into the country of another
person's suffering? Have someone else's wounds
opened a trap door into your own deeps?

Traditional ideas of effective leadership are under question today. In an article in the *Yale Alumni Magazine* entitled "Success: Who Needs It?" the author, Ren Frutkin, says, "What Yale's 'male leaders' no longer want to be is male leaders." He details a revolt from machismo style; aggressive, cool, unemotional leadership. He adds, "Even the hallowed notion of service has come under scrutiny. The 'helping' professions—law, medicine, divinity —are questioned as possible ego-traps. For some people, deciding to go into these professions can be socially disastrous: there is an ugly tendency to force everyone you come in contact with into needing your help. The aggressive, typically masculine attitudes needed for success can produce blunt, one-sided people. 'If you only have a hammer,' says one psychiatrist, 'then everything you deal with is a nail.' " [9]

I have personally experienced the disabilities felt by both the giver and the receiver of a personal transaction when the giver believes that it is his task to give, but not his need also to receive. That is just as degrading for a relationship as for a receiver to feel that it is his prerogative to receive but not his responsibility to give.

Frutkin quotes Robert Jay Lifton as saying that

two of the important qualities of the new leadership needed today will be vulnerability and a certain kind of humor. "Vulnerability," he says, "captures and reflects and in some ways furthers our struggle with our own overwhelmingly visible frailties. But mockery and self-mockery have also become essential to leadership, because one needs not only humor but mockery to evoke the depth of our problems and the lack of fit between where we are and where we have to go. I really distrust those who are totally without humor and totally unyielding in their claim to certainty." [10]

Self-mockery lends distance to vulnerability, avoiding self-pity. Vulnerability lends warmth and caring to self-mockery, avoiding cynicism or sarcasm. Vulnerability needs a Mona Lisa secret smile which seems to say that things are never as bad as we think they are, and never as good either.

I have had personal experiences recently related both to a lawyer and a psychologist. I was their client in each case, and both were helping me. The role was clear. Yet the role did not prevent a genuine human exchange from taking place, nor did it impinge on my dignity as a client or receiver nor did it impede the personal involvement and sharing in some degree of the giver. Our wounds, handled wisely and tenderly and with some humor, can be bridges of mutual communication and revelation.

It is an amazing grace, I think, that our wounds are also a major source of healing power for others. A Christmas letter was written some years ago by an older couple in First Community Village. It is entitled "A Final Greeting":

> It has been a fetish with our family since the later 1920's to send out Christmas cards that make some claim of originality. Our relatives have advised us to attempt no card this Christmas due to our health. So, as our farewell Season's Greetings, we are writing this letter.
>
> As one becomes an octogenarian, more and more is heard of the Harvest Years, the Golden Years, or as Robert Browning expresses it: "Grow old along with me! The best is yet to be, the last of life for which the first was made!" This is all very well until you see your high school sweetheart with whom you have spent fifty-seven years, gasping for breath and a physician coming once a week to inject a fluid into her veins to ease that breathing. Then it is that one can easily become a believer

in euthanasia. We have landed a man on the
moon, but not yet are we wise enough to
practice this art of compassion.

We close our last Christmas message to you
with words adapted from Max Ehrmann:
"We have a few friends who have loved us for
what we are and we try to keep ever burning
before our vagrant steps the kindly light of
hope. Though age and infirmity have overtaken
us and we have not yet come within sight of
the castle of our dreams, may we still be
thankful for time's old memories that are good
and sweet; and may the evening's twilight
find us gentle still." [11]

The wounded heart of that letter enables us to
feel our own wounds and provides a healing flow
for us as well.

In sharing our wounds, the healing power is
released. We learn that he who would bind another's
wounds must allow his own wounds to be bound.
God has only one kind of healer in this world—a
wounded healer. I resist baring my wounds. For
many years I even resisted acknowledging to
myself, much less to anyone else, that I had
wounds. I learned to evade my inner ache by
externalizing myself. Only in recent years have
I been allowing my wounds to see the light of day.

Not long ago I was talking with a friend and
colleague about a rupture in relationship with
someone in the congregation. It had not been
possible to mend the rupture. We talked about the
sorrow and sadness of hurting another person—of
being hurt—and somehow being unable to get
across that gulf. As I was sharing this little wound
I suddenly felt my heart coming up into my throat.
I had to turn away for a while to keep my tears
to myself. After I regained my composure we
concluded our conversation. Later in the day, I
found on my desk a handwritten note from this
person which reads in part: "Dear Bob, My heart
ached and I was moved deeply by the pain you were
feeling this morning and I know you have felt
on other occasions. I don't really know how to
comfort you, but want you to know that I pray for
you, love you and support you to the fullest
extent of my being. May you be healed,
strengthened, blessed, made whole, may you be
persistent and your vision kept clear, and may
you know that you are loved as a beautiful, truly
beautiful, human being."

I don't expect to receive a more healing
benediction in my lifetime than that one. And it
wouldn't have been given to me except that, for a

moment, I was unable to hide my wounds. A
moment long enough for someone to see and care,
and in the caring, healing began to happen.

Our primary task in our life together, as Nouwen
puts it, is not to take away pain but to deepen it
to "a level where it can be shared." [12] In the
sharing is the healing. We are not to be ashamed
of our wounds nor proud of them, but simply willing
to acknowledge them and to share them and to
recognize them as signs of hope.

Nouwen says, ". . . the wound, which causes us to
suffer now, will be revealed to us later as the place
where God intimated his new creation." [13] That's
really good news, isn't it! It is the promise that
in our every darkness a light continues to shine
and that we learn through failure, losing and hurting
what health, winning and success really are. Love
is our wound, and as long as we love, we will be
wounded, and our wounds are indeed the places
where God keeps intimating his new creation.

In Alexander Solzhenitsyn's novel *Cancer Ward*,
Oleg Kostoglotov survives months in a cancer
ward. During the period of his suffering, he distills
the trivialities of his life down to its essence. The
day comes when he is well enough to leave the
hospital, and for Oleg it is nothing less than

resurrection. For us, too, suffering as we may be
in the cancer wards of our own lives, his experience
may signal the health and hope that are coming.

> Early in the morning . . . Oleg got up
> quietly. . . . It was the morning of creation.
> The world had been created anew for one
> reason only, to be given back to Oleg. "Go out
> and live!" it seemed to say. . . . His face radiated
> happiness . . . with that early-morning
> springtime joy that touches even the old and
> sick. . . .
> The first morning of creation . . . [Oleg]
> conceived the mad scheme of going to the Old
> Town immediately, while it was still early
> morning, to look at a flowering apricot tree. He
> walked through the forbidden gates [got on
> a trolley to the Old Town and looked at people
> on the trolley as though they were the first
> human beings he had ever seen. He got off,
> walked down a side street, stopped at a
> teahouse, sat down and began to sip his tea.]
> And then from the teahouse balcony he saw
> above the walled courtyard next door
> something pink and transparent. It looked
> like a puff dandelion, only it was six meters
> in diameter, a rosy, weightless balloon. He'd
> never seen anything so pink and so huge. . . .
> He walked up to the railings and from on high
> gazed and gazed through this pink miracle.

It was his present to himself—his creation-day present.

It was like a fire tree decorated with candles. . . . The flowering apricot was the only tree in this courtyard . . . open to the sky. . . . Oleg examined it—pinkness, that was the general impression. The tree had buds like candles. When on the point of opening, the petals were pink in color, but once open they were pure white, like apple or cherry blossoms. The result was an incredible, tender pink. Oleg was trying to absorb it all into his eyes. He wanted to remember it for a long time. . . . He'd planned on finding a miracle, and he had found one.[14]

There's a pink miracle waiting for you and me too on the first morning of our becoming a new creation.

Notes

Chapter 1

1. Dale Tarnowieski, *The Changing Success Ethic, An AMA Survey Report* (AMACOM 1973), p. 7.
2. Ibid., p. 4.
3. 2 Cor. 5:17, RSV.
4. Barbara Fried, *The Middle Age Crisis* (New York: Harper & Row, 1967), pp. 130, 5. To be reissued by Harper & Row in paperback in Spring 1976, with an introduction by Robert A. Raines.
5. Erik Erikson, *Childhood and Society* (New York: W. W. Norton & Company, Inc., 1950).
6. John 3:1–8, RSV.
7. Quoted with permission of Richard C. Raines, Jr., from letter to his parents, June 8, 1968.
8. John C. Raines, *Attack on Privacy* (Valley Forge: Judson Press, 1974), pp. 55, 72.
9. Dr. W. Hugh Missildine is a psychiatrist in Columbus, Ohio, and author of *Your Inner Child of the Past* (New York: Simon and Schuster, 1963).

147

10. Letter from Barbara Moore, Columbus, Ohio, teacher and member of First Community Church.
11. Paraphrased from Rom. 8:33–34.
12. Lorraine Hansberry, *The Sign in Sidney Brustein's Window* (New York: Signet Books), pp. 316–18.

Chapter 2

1. Margaret R. Weiss, "Creative Vision, Six Decades of the Photographic Art," *Saturday Review*, September 22, 1962, p. 53.
2. Luke 4:18–19, RSV.
3. William Saroyan, *The Human Comedy* (New York: Harcourt, Brace and Company, 1943), pp. 287–288.
4. Eph. 4:13, RSV.
5. Elie Wiesel, *Souls on Fire* (New York: Random House, 1972), in review by Charles Silberman in *The New York Times Book Review*, March 5, 1972.
6. The Power and Light Program was designed by John and Adrienne Carr, members of the program staff of First Community Church. These materials will be published by the United Methodist Church in 1975. Further information may be obtained by writing to The Reverend John L. Carr, First Community Church, 1320 Cambridge Boulevard, Columbus, Ohio 43212.
7. Ps. 103:1–5, KJV.
8. Ps. 103:2–4, 8, 13.
9. Forbes Robinson, *Letters to His Friends* (London: Spottiswoode & Co. Ltd., 1904), pp. 44–46.
10. Rene Dubos, *A God Within* (New York: Charles Scribner's Sons, 1972), pp. 6–7.
11. Ibid., pp. 10–11.
12. Persons and places to write about such meditative

processes include: The Reverend L. Robert Keck, Prayer and Meditation Research Project, First Community Church, 1320 Cambridge Boulevard, Columbus, Ohio 43212; Dr. Ira Progoff, Dialogue House Associates, Inc., 45 West Tenth Street, New York City, New York 10011; Dr. John E. Biersdorf, Institute for Advanced Pastoral Studies, 380 Lone Pine Road, P.O. Box 809, Bloomfield Hills, Michigan 48013; Father Henri Nouwen, Yale Divinity School, New Haven, Connecticut 06510; Kirkridge, Inc., Bangor, Pennsylvania 18013.

13. Dubos, p. 83.
14. Robert Jay Lifton, "The Struggle for Cultural Rebirth," *Harper's Magazine*, April 1973, p. 88.

Chapter 3

1. Peter Schrag, *The End of the American Future* (New York: Simon & Schuster, 1973), in column by Norman Nadel, Scripps-Howard Staff Writer, *Citizen-Journal*, Columbus, Ohio, date unavailable.
2. John C. Raines, "Middle America: Up Against the Wall and Going Nowhere," *The Christian Century*, May 2, 1973, pp. 504–507. An additional reference is an article in *The New York Times*, December 16, 1974, p. 57, headlined "Most Stock Found Still Owned By Rich": "The richest two-tenths of 1 percent of Americans owned 30 percent of all the stock as of mid-1971. The richest 1 percent owned just over half of it. These were two of the findings of one of the most comprehensive studies ever made of stock ownership, which was published last week in the November issue of the Commerce Department's Survey of Current Business."

3. Robert Dietsch, Scripps-Howard staff writer, *Citizen-Journal*, Columbus, Ohio, April 15, 1974, p. 19.

4. Paraphrased from Ephesians 2:14–15.

5. Alistair Cooke, "Letter to America," *House and Garden*, February 1974, pp. 52–53.

6. Henry Steele Commager, "The Constitution Is Alive and Well," *The New York Times*, August 11, 1974, p. E17. © 1974 by The New York Times Company. Reprinted by permission.

7. Kenneth Clark, *Civilisation* (New York: Harper & Row, 1969), p. 4.

8. Isa. 40:1–2, 31, RSV.

9. James Reston, Convocation Day address, Ohio State University, printed in *The Ohio State University Monthly*, May 1970, pp. 12–13. © 1970 by The New York Times Company. Reprinted by permission.

10. Jon Nordheimer, "The 'New South' Is No Longer a Slogan; It's a Description," *The New York Times*, December 30, 1973, p. E5. © 1973 by The New York Times Company. Reprinted by permission.

11. David Hackworth, "A Soldier's Case for Total Amnesty," *Chicago Tribune*, August 4, 1974, sec. 2, p. 1. Reprinted courtesy of *The Chicago Tribune*.

12. Ps. 103:8, 10–12, RSV.

13. Matt. 6:12, 14–15, RSV.

14. See Isa. 10:5–11.

15. Anthony Lewis, "Happy Birthday," *The New York Times*, July 5, 1973, p. 29. © 1973 by The New York Times Company. Reprinted by permission.

16. Carl Sandburg, "The People Speak," *The People, Yes* (New York: Harcourt, Brace & Company, 1936).

Chapter 4

1. Sidney Lovett, "People," *Sports Illustrated,* February 5, 1973, p. 50.
2. William Blake, *Auguries of Innocence,* Ib.
3. James Reston, *The New York Times,* in Elisabeth D. Dodds, *Voices of Protest and Hope* (New York: Friendship Press, 1965), pp. 145–146.

Chapter 5

1. Georges Bernanos, *The Diary of a Country Priest* (New York: Doubleday & Company, Inc., Image Books, 1937), p. 22.
2. Pierre Teilhard de Chardin, *The Divine Milieu* (New York: Harper & Brothers, Publishers, 1960), p. 58.

Chapter 6

1. Henri J. M. Nouwen, *The Wounded Healer* (New York: Doubleday & Company, Inc., 1972), p. 86.
2. Ibid., pp. 86–87.
3. Jer. 8:18–22, RSV.
4. 1 Cor. 2:1–5, TEV.
5. Theodore Roethke, *Words for the Wind* (Bloomington: Indiana University Press, 1932), p. 210.
6. Ibid., p. 143.
7. Luke 9:58, RSV.
8. Nouwen, p. 86.

9. Ren Frutkin, "Success: Who Needs It?," *Yale Alumni Magazine,* June 1971, p. 10.
10. Ibid., p. 11.
11. Christmas letter written in 1972 by Lester and Ethel Black, residents of First Community Village, Columbus, Ohio.
12. Nouwen, p. 94.
13. Ibid., p. 98.
14. Alexander Solzhenitsyn, *Cancer Ward* (New York: Grosset and Dunlap, Inc., Bantam Books, 1968), pp. 484–490.